REASON AND REALITY

John Polkinghorne

REASON AND REALITY

The Relationship between Science and Theology

TRINITY PRESS INTERNATIONAL

Valley Forge, PA

First Trinity Press International Edition 1991

Trinity Press International
P.O. Box 851
Valley Forge, PA 19482

To the Fellows and Scholars of Queens' College, Cambridge, from their President

Library of Congress Cataloging-in-Publication Data
Polkinghorne, J.C., 1930-
Reason and reality : the relationship between science and theology / John Polkinghorne.
    p.   cm.
    Includes bibliographical references and index.
ISBN 1-56338-019-6
    1. Religion and science—1946-   I. Title
BL241.P57 1991
261.5'5—dc20   91-23518
                                          CIP

Printed in the United States of America
95 96 97 98 6 5 4 3 2

Begin with God from the bottom upwards, not from the top downwards.

MARTIN LUTHER

Contents

Acknowledgements

Chapters 1 to 3 are based on the Riddell Lectures which I gave in the University of Newcastle in 1990. Chapter 4 is based on my Warburton Lecture to the Honourable Society of Lincoln's Inn in 1990. Chapter 6 is based on a lecture given at Gresham College in 1991. In each case I am grateful for the invitation to speak and for hospitality received.

I wish to thank Dr Mary Tanner for some helpful comments; my wife Ruth for help in correcting the proofs; and the editorial staff of SPCK for their assistance in preparing the manuscript for press.

John Polkinghorne
Queens' College,
Cambridge

Introduction

I have written three short books[1] which together seek to survey issues relating to science and theology. The writing was concise, partly because that is my style and partly because the aim was to be accessible to the general reader who sought an overview of this area of intellectual activity. I do not think that brevity was purchased at the expense of academic seriousness, but there were certainly matters raised which would bear further consideration, not least in the light of continuing reflection on the questions involved. The present book of essays (based partly on invited lectures) gives me an opportunity to return to some of these issues.

Most of the writers in the science-theology debate approach the matter from an intellectual experience formed initially within science, and only with subsequent involvement in theology. It is a matter of regret that, with some honourable exceptions, so little attention has been paid to these matters by those whose formation was theological.[2] To the scientists exploring theology it has often seemed that there is a kinship between the two disciplines. Chapter 1 considers this claim. It emphasizes that neither science nor theology can be pursued without a measure of intellectual daring, for neither is based on incontrovertible grounds of knowledge. Yet both can, I believe, lay claim to achieving a critical realism. Each demands commitment to a corrigible point of view as a necessary starting-point in the search for truth. Each has to be open to the way things are and must conform its mode of inquiry to the nature of the reality it encounters (a point repeatedly emphasized by Tom Torrance,[3] one of the 'honourable exceptions'). It has been said that science uses 'universe-assisted logic';[4] theology must employ 'liturgy-assisted logic'.

Both theology and science have to speak of entities which are not directly observable. In consequence, both must be prepared to make use of model and metaphor. Chapter 2 explores this theme. It begins with an analysis of the use of models in contemporary physics, from which I conclude that they are frankly heuristic devices and are to be distinguished from a theory, which is a candidate for the verisimilitudinous description of what is actually the case. In consequence, a variety of (possibly contradictory) models is tolerable, because of their limited domains

1

of applicability, but the ambitious aim of a theory demands that it should be unique. Theology, because of the difficulty of its task, is unlikely to achieve more than a collection of viable models, usable with discretion. Mathematics is the natural language of physical science; symbol, because of its poetic openness of meaning, proves to be the natural language of theology.

A recurrent theme in writings on science and theology is that of antireductionism. Taking science seriously should not lead us to believe that the world is 'nothing but' a collection of elementary particles. The conventional antireductionist argument maintains that we must recognize the validity of the upward emergence of novelty (so that biology is more than physics writ large, etc.) Chapter 3 suggests that this insight needs complementing by the recognition also of the possibility of downward emergence (so that elementary particle physics itself may be a kind of approximation to a more subtle and supple physical reality). I believe that the modern theory of exquisitely sensitive dynamical systems (rather inaptly called 'the theory of chaos') offers an important clue to how this might be so, leading to the possibility of a degree of understanding of how both ourselves and God may act in the world. I reject criticisms that this account of divine interaction might prove a return to the God of the gaps. Instead, I maintain that its picture of information-flow is a plausible way of making sense of otherwise unsubstantiated claims of a downward-acting causation, either human or divine.

To some, science appears reasonable, open to correction in the light of what actually happens, whilst religion seems ever ready to play the trump card of unquestionable revelation in order to curtail further rational argument. Chapter 4 rejects this picture. It sees revelation as the record of particularly transparent moments of encounter with the Divine, not the issuing of guaranteed and unchallengeable propositions.

Much as I respect Newton and Maxwell, I do not find myself continually returning to a perusal of the *Principia* or the *Treatise on Electricity and Magnetism*. Yet the Bible continues to play a normative role in Christian thinking. Is there not a great contrast between the openness of science to new ideas and the enslavement of theology to the entail of Scripture? Chapter 5 discusses the use of the Bible and defends its continuing validity, not only as evidence for the foundational events of the tradition but also as a 'classic' of ever-contemporary significance. An important concept is John Barton's notion of the 'semantic indeterminacy of sacred texts',[5] which delivers us from too narrow a construal of their meaning and significance. The chapter ends with a brief survey of scriptural passages of relevance to the science-theology debate.

Chapter 6 is concerned with content, the interaction between the descriptions of the world proffered by science and by theology. The cross-traffic across the border is held not to be symmetrical in the two directions. Because theology speaks of God it necessarily has to try to embrace the insights of all forms of human inquiry and to place them within the most comprehensive and profound setting available. Thus it offers science the possibility of an answer to those meta-questions arising from the latter, but which are beyond science's own ability to discuss. Science, on the other hand, offers theology knowledge of what the physical world is really like, in its history and nature, thereby imposing conditions of consonance which theology must respect in giving its account of God and his creation. The chapter gives examples and discussion of these contrasting forms of interaction.

The biggest revolution in physical thought since the days of Newton has been brought about by the discovery of the elusive and fitful subatomic world of quantum theory. Chapter 7 considers what general lessons of interest to theology might arise from this intellectual upheaval. Everyday reasonableness is seen not to be the measure of all things; the world has proved strange beyond our powers of anticipation. If that is true for physics, it is doubtless true for theology as well. The quantum world exhibits a counterintuitive non-locality, a togetherness-in-separation, which provides a powerful image of holistic solidarity which might be of value to theologians and which is certainly much more fitting for that purpose than is the mere notion of a field, to which some have assigned mistaken significance. The chapter does not assume knowledge of the formalism of quantum mechanics, but it will inevitably make demands upon its readers, for the subject is one whose concepts, at first encounter, are very surprising to us. One of the most important lessons from the story of quantum theory is the encouragement to be open to the totally unexpected, even to the initially apparently unintelligible.

The final brief chapter seeks to use some of the insights of the preceding discussion to consider the Christian doctrine I find the most perplexing: the notion of the Fall and its eschatological reversal. It is an exercise attempting to take both scientific understanding and Christian tradition with an equal seriousness.

1 Rational Inquiry

The idea that science and theology might be intellectual cousins under the skin has been proposed by a number of recent writers. The mathematician J. R. Carnes assures us that theology 'stands in exactly the same relation to religious experience as scientific theory does to our ordinary experience of the world'.[1] Ian Barbour [2] compares a religious world view to a scientific paradigm (in the sense of Kuhn[3]) or a scientific research programme (in the sense of Lakatos[4]). Both science and theology involve the acceptance of a broad interpretative framework which is neither impervious to experience nor vulnerable to ready falsification by it. It may at times seem that the religious apologist is too nimble with his excuses for the ills of a world held to be the creation of a benevolent God, but equally the physicist, believing matter to be made up of quarks and gluons but invoking the property of 'confinement' to explain their non-appearance in the laboratory,[5] is also displaying the ability to save a good idea in the face of what might have seemed a straightforward negation of it. Barbour assigns science and theology to different positions within a common ' "falsifiability" spectrum',[6] with neither being at the extreme of completely immediate objectivity or the extreme of complete invulnerability to evidence. A similar view is taken by Arthur Peacocke, who defends a critical realist philosophy in both science and theology, saying:

> the scientific and theological enterprises share alike the tools of groping humanity - our stock of words, ideas and images that have been handed down, tools that we refashion in our own way for our own times in the light of experiment and experience to relate to the natural world and that are available, with God's guidance, to steer our own paths from birth to death.[7]

Finally, my own earlier attempt to compare science and theology led me to the conclusion that they 'have this in common, that each can be, and should be, defended as being investigations of what is, the search for increasing verisimilitude in our understanding of reality'.[8]

The writers referred to so far are all scientists with strong theological interests, who might well be expected to incline to assimilating science and theology to each other. However, some

4

of those firmly based within the theological community itself have expressed similar ideas. It is a major theme of the writings of Thomas Torrance. He speaks of an 'interrogative form of inquiry' which is 'directed ultimately to the self-disclosure of the object' and which must 'always involve the leap forward to be obedient to the new as it is allowed to disclose itself... In natural science this is spoken of as *discovery*, in theology this is spoken of as *revelation*, the difference between discovery and revelation being determined by the nature of the object with which each has to do'.[9] Bernard Lonergan said that 'Mathematics, science, philosophy, ethics, theology differ in many manners; but they have the common factor that their objectivity is the fruit of alertness, intelligence, reasonableness and responsibility'[10] qualities whose pursuit corresponds to what Lonergan called the transcendental method 'concerned with meeting the exigencies and exploiting the opportunities presented by the human mind itself'.[11] Wolfhart Pannenberg seeks to speak of theology as the 'Science of God' which 'would then mean the study of the totality of the real from the point of view of the reality which ultimately determines it both as a whole and in its parts'.[12]

The underlying thought is that of a rational inquiry into what our experience leads us to believe is actually the case. Even for science this is a claim that has been hotly disputed.[13] The underdetermination of theory by experiment, the revolutionary character of some scientific change (as when Newton gave way to Einstein and Heisenberg), the insights of the sociology of knowledge into the existence of perspectives imposed by communal expectation, all these have been held to dispose of naive claims that science is about the way the world is. Many are not prepared to concede to it more than an instrumental success, the attainment of manners of speaking which are effective in getting things done but which are not to be taken with ontological seriousness. Science has not been immune from the acid attack of the hermeneutics of suspicion, so characteristic of the thought of the last hundred years.

Yet it is from the sidelines that these sceptical voices are raised. Very few of those actually engaged in scientific work doubt that they are learning about the actual pattern and process of the physical world. Indeed it would otherwise be hard to understand how instrumental success could be attained so consistently if there were not a significant degree of verisimilitude in the scientific account of the world. I do not want to fight that particular battle again, having already manned the critical realist redoubt in another engagement.[14] That defence occurred in the course of a review of the development of elementary particle physics in the period

1950-80, which I wished to interpret as the *discovery* of the quark structure of matter, not merely its socially agreed construction.[15] In my view, such an historical framework is essential for the discussion of the philosophy of science. I am in great sympathy with the assertion of Ernan McMullin that 'realism... is in part an empirical thesis'.[16] The issue will never be settled by logical analysis alone but it requires us to look and see if we have experiential grounds for its acceptance. As McMullin says:

> Scientific realism is not a doctrine about the implications of successful retroductive inference. Nor is it a metaphysical claim about how the world *must* be. It has both logical and metaphysical components. It is a quite limited claim that purports to explain why certain ways of proceeding in science have worked out as well as they (contingently) have.[17]

The beguiling notion that we can, by seeking clear and certain ideas, construct from thought alone an impregnable metaphysic, seems to me to be a delusion. Our rational inquiry has to include a response to what we experience, for it stands in need of what David Park has called 'universe-assisted logic: although there is much about the universe that we do not know, the universe is such that it allows us to make certain useful definitions and draw certain conclusions'.[18] We need this assistance. The poor record of achievement of those from Plato through Descartes to Kant and beyond who have taken a contrary view, does nothing to discourage this attitude of looking-and-seeing. Lessing's criticism of a historically-based theology – that 'Accidental truths of history can never become the proof of necessary truths of reason' – cuts little ice with a scientist, who is not disposed to grant much power to unassisted reason.

Though certainty would be welcome, Gödel has taught us that even mathematics requires an act of commitment as to its ultimate consistency, and other forms of intellectual inquiry are surely going to have their own form of precariousness. Because we can only approach reality from some initial point of view, experience and interpretation are inevitably intertwined. We cannot escape from the hermeneutic circle. In Paul Ricoeur's words: 'The circle can be stated bluntly: "We must understand in order to believe but we must believe in order to understand" '.[19] The scientist commits himself to belief in the rationality of the world in order to discover what form that rationality takes. His success should encourage others to similar boldness. One might put it in theological terms by saying that the image of God is not so defaced in humanity that we are unable to attain a verisimilitudinous grasp of reality. A certain intellectual courage is called for, 'a frame of mind in which I hold firmly to what I believe to be true, even though I know that it might conceivably be false'.[20] The achievement of such a point of view was what Michael Polanyi described as being his principal purpose in writing *Personal Knowledge*. Boldness, however, must not become foolhardiness. The possibility of correction must always be entertained, though not to the point of intellectual paralysis, for while 'The possibility of error is a necessary element of any belief bearing on reality... to withhold belief on the grounds of such a hazard is to break off all contact with reality'.[21] A physicist would find his own natural phrase to describe the hermeneutic circle. He would call it 'the intellectual bootstrap',[22] the necessary self-sustaining act by which a world of understanding is held in being, the recognition that 'Any enquiry into our ultimate beliefs can be consistent only if it presupposes its own conclusions. It must be intentionally circular.'[23]

Oddly enough, those who have been most insistent in their criticism of claims to rationality nevertheless themselves tacitly recognize this need for intellectual boldness in our address to the world. The Freudian claiming that he can exhibit the unconscious sexual motivations of our thought, the Marxist who believes he can lay bare its class and economic basis, the deconstructionist asserting that the text has no particular meaning, all imply an exemption for themselves. The hermeneutic suspicion expressed in such reductionist criticism would always be self-defeating if it did not have recourse to an understood saving-clause in its own favour. Each must have the nerve to spring his own trap by believing that he has some access to truth about what is going on. No one of serious intent can escape the necessity of an intellectual bootstrap to raise himself above the earthbound state of unreflective experience.

If that is true, one may ask what will prevent the construction of a plurality of understandings, each sustained by its own originating act of commitment? It will not be long before someone draws our attention to people like the Azande tribe, whose account of a world of witchcraft possesses its own inner consistency without most of us feeling able to embrace it.[24] We are right to resist. Our preference for a biochemical explanation for the poisonous action of 'benge', rather than its explanation in oracular terms, is entirely rational, since it forms part of a much wider explanatory framework incorporating many phenomena excluded from consideration by the Azande. It is the satisfaction of very general criteria, such as comprehensiveness, simplicity, and fertility in further development, which should be the distinguishing mark of a truly rational inquiry.

Rationality is very much more than correct deduction. It incorporates the skilful assessment of qualities such as simplicity and naturalness of explanation, which cannot be given exhaustive prior characterization but which have to be perceived intuitively. Scientific progress depends upon the fruitful exercise of induction, another example of that unformalizable tacit skill about which Polanyi wrote so extensively. ('We know more than we can tell.') Who can specify precisely how many instances must be examined before a natural law is held to be substantiated? Yet the history of science abundantly supports the view that this skill can be exercised successfully, leading to well-defined understanding of the physical world, agreed throughout the scientific community. I do not believe that the unanimity with which well-winnowed scientific theories are accepted is just a measure of the socially-induced suggestibility of the scientist. People often strive for novel ways of looking at old data, as the young seek to assert themselves against the received wisdom of their elders, thereby hoping to establish their own reputations. Their labours do not throw up a plethora of alternative theories. Something like the quark theory of matter, or big bang cosmology, is a complex construction accommodating great varieties of data within a scheme of understanding controlled by general physical principles such as relativistic quantum theory or general relativity. There seems to be no reason whatsoever to suppose that there are alternative interpretative schemes of comparable generality which have just been overlooked. The repeated convergence of physical theory upon agreed solutions is prime evidence for a critical realist position and a strong encouragement to undertake the risk of an 'intellectual bootstrap' in the pursuit of rational inquiry into the way things are.

By now the theologian may be feeling distinctly uneasy. It is all very well to invoke the lessons of history in defence of critical realism in science, but does not history tell us a very different story when we come to consider theology? Even within a single religion we have persisting and conflicting traditions – the principle of *sola scriptura* against the magisterium of the Church, Calvinism versus Arminianism, liberal against conservative, and so on – and when we lift our eyes from Christianity to survey the world's religions the degree of dissonance greatly increases. It is this very fact that encourages many thoughtful people to accept science as dealing with public fact but to relegate religion to a ghetto of private opinion.

I believe the answer to lie in the recognition that science is easy and theology hard, because of the greatly differing degrees of control and power to interrogate that each exercises over the object of its inquiry. The physical world is at our disposal to prod or pull apart as we please. The successes of science are purchased by the modesty of its ambition, its self-limiting definition as concerned with certain impersonal and largely repeatable aspects of experience. Within science, the most comprehensively successful explanatory schemes are to be found in those subjects with the least degree of complexity. Physics is more successful in this way than biology, because it tackles an easier task; elementary particle physics and cosmology are among the most successful branches of physics because they investigate regimes whose extreme characters (very small or very large) produce a further degree of simplification. If one day the fundamental physicists find the master equations of a grand unified theory (a Theory of Everything capable of being written on a T-shirt, as they say in their hubristic way) the result will be gratifying but strictly limited. The consequences of those equations for the behaviour of systems of any degree of complexity would be an immensely challenging task which would call for different techniques from those used in the preceding basic investigation.[25] Stephen Hawking has suggested that the discovery of a grand unified theory would lead to an understanding of why the universe exists and so to 'the ultimate triumph of human reason – for we should know the mind of God'.[26] The claim is rhetorically extravagant and philosophically dubious, for the achievement would only be the beginning of an understanding of physics itself, let alone more complicated aspects of reality. There is more to the mind of God than physics will ever disclose.

As our rational inquiry moves us from the simplicities of physical science to the complexities of personal experience and on to the mystery of encounter with the divine, its increasing difficulty is likely to be reflected in a loss of convergence on to universally agreed understandings. Not only will cultural factors play a larger part in forming those 'spectacles behind the eyes' through which we view the world, but dependence on tacit skills of judgement will increase as the power of manipulative testing decreases. Even within physics, with all its experimental capability, there are issues which can only be settled in this way. Conventional quantum theory describes a world intrinsically cloudy and fitful in its behaviour. It understands Heisenberg's uncertainty principle as expressing a genuine indeterminacy. There is an alternative account due to David Bohm which asserts quantum events to be perfectly determined but by factors partially beyond our knowledge. It understands the uncertainty principle to be no more than an expression of our ignorance.[27] These two theories lead to identical experimental consequences, so that they cannot be discriminated empirically. Yet the great majority of physicists hold to the former because it seems to them to be more natural and economic than Bohm's clever construct. That judgement, which I share, goes beyond a mere satisfaction of empirical adequacy and invokes, quite properly, wider criteria. To recognize this is not to make quantum physics irrational but simply to accept that our concept of rational motivation will have to be wide enough to accommodate acts of judgement of a kind that made Polanyi talk about science as 'personal knowledge'. The exercise of reason is the activity of persons and it cannot be delegated to computers, however cleverly programmed. We know more than we can tell.

Considerations of this kind clearly become more weighty as we move into realms of more personal experience. As a result, the possibilities for disagreement about how best to essay the intellectual bootstrap increase. Religious traditions are organized around normative figures (Jesus, Muhammad, Buddha) and give high esteem to certain writings accorded the status of Scripture (the Bible, the Koran, the Pali Canon). The recognition that there are these very different starting-points for religious understanding should not make us despair of theological inquiry, any more than the difference between Bohr and Bohm should make us abandon investigation of the quantum world. In each case there is a reality (God, the subatomic world) whose nature we are seeking to explore. The variety of the world's religions warns us of the difficulty of the theological task but it does not prohibit a rational inquiry in which the seeker adopts 'a frame of mind in which I hold firmly to what I believe even though I know it might conceivably be false'. In theological terms, this is to walk by faith and not by sight. In ecumenical terms, this is the stance I must adopt in my encounter with those of a differing faith, both respectful to the insights they offer and firm in adherence to what I have been able to make my own. In intellectual terms, it is to recognize that I never approach reality with my mind a mere *tabula rasa*, awaiting impressions, but my inquiry is always conducted from a (potentially corrigible) initial point of view.

We have noted that even within a religious tradition there are considerable differences of opinion. A Christian theologian, Stephen Sykes, has suggested that this is necessary:

Not merely is conflict inherent in the early days of the Christian movement, it is inherent in the very existence of the Christian Church at every stage of its life... Conflict arises because there is real difficulty in determining the proper relationship between the internal dimension of Christian commitment, and decisions or teaching about its diverse external dimensions.[28]

In other words, internal spiritual experience cannot readily, or with unanimity, find its expression in outward communication. Here indeed is an area of human life where we know more than we can tell.

The picture I am developing is of theology placed within an area of human discourse where science also finds a home. Rational inquiry is not characterized by an unwillingness to take intellectual risks, so that we cling alone to what is deductively certain, but it is bold enough to venture on the construction of a metaphysical scheme whose justification will lie in its attainment of comprehensive explanatory power. The success of science should encourage us to take such a bet on the reasonableness of the world and commit ourselves to an openness of experience to being understood. If our search is for the most comprehensive account of reality and we exclude tidy oversimplifications obtained by truncating the variety of experience, then in this endeavour we shall not need to make a stark choice between the coherence theory of truth (I believe because it all hangs together) and the correspondence theory of truth (I believe because it is the case) – that is, provided we understand coherence as including consonance with phenomena, not just the self-contained consistency of a formal scheme. Without that proviso there might well be a variety of options (Riemannian geometry of curved space is as coherent as the Euclidean geometry of flat space, but only one will fit the facts). With that proviso, the critical realist believes the way things are will provide the necessary clue to how they are to be understood. Those who commit themselves to this trust in a rational cosmos are asserting intelligibility to be the key to reality. (I have elsewhere argued that this is the basis on which the quantum physicist should defend his belief in the reality of the elusive inhabitants of his unpicturable world.[29]) Of course there is no absolute necessity about this point of view; its adoption can only be as a contingent piece of universe-assisted logic. I believe that assistance to be available and that we are encouraged to pursue a programme of rational inquiry. That encouragement is itself a striking fact about the world which can lead to a version of the cosmological argument for God's existence.[30] This was put in lapidary form by Bernard Lonergan: 'If the real is completely intelligible, then God exists. But the real is completely intelligible. Therefore God exists'.[31]

What I am rejecting is foundationalism, the Cartesian search for a totally secure basis on which to construct knowledge. This latter view encourages a propositional account of theology, seen as the development of the consequences of dogmatic formulae guaranteed by an unchallengeable authority (whether the deliverances of the human mind, or Scripture, or tradition, or simply revelation). It is a defect of Carnes' notion of the relationship of science and theology[32] that he gives just such an axiomatic account of both disciplines. John Puddefoot rightly calls this view misleading

> because it treats axioms, whether in mathematics or theology, as givens, as if axioms themselves have no history... This locates the roots of systems in quite the wrong place: an axiom set is not the foundation of a system, but the product of generations of mathematical enquiry as it has eventually been formalized or *axiomatized*.[33]

This failure to reckon with where the axioms have come from, to take due account of their distillation from experience, Puddefoot called 'the sin of retrospective refinement'. The result is a spurious air of certitude, the kind of claim against which Einstein protested in the case of physics when he made his famous remark that 'as far as the propositions of mathematics relate to reality they are not certain and as far as they are certain they do not relate to reality'.[34] Alasdair MacIntyre draws a similar distinction in his account of the thought of Thomas Aquinas, distinguishing between 'rational justification within a science, the rational justification of a science, and the rational justification required by an account of the sciences as a whole, hierarchically ordered system'. Within a science deductive argument is used by Aquinas but 'First principles will be dialectically justifiable'.[35] Hence Aquinas's use of the dialectic method of objection and reply (with its implication of openness to possible further development) in tackling the basic issues of the *Summa Theologiae*.

George Lindbeck assures us that to reject foundationalism is not necessarily to embrace relativism but simply to recognize that there is no logically neutral ground from which to judge. We have to approach reality from a point of view, judiciously chosen and continuously reassessed. We cannot avoid trying on some kind of spectacles behind the eyes. 'Thus reasonableness in religion and theology, as in other domains, has something of that aesthetic character, that quality of unformalizable skill, which we usually associate with the artist or the linguistically competent'.[36] We are back in Polanyi country, knowing more than we can tell, successfully exercising tacit skills.

Lindbeck outlines three possible approaches to theology. The first is cognitive, involving claims to knowledge. He regards its characteristic style as propositional. The second is experiential-expressive, concerned with doctrines as symbols denoting inner attitudes. The third, which is his own preference, he calls cultural-linguistic. 'The function of church doctrines which becomes most prominent in this perspective is their use, not as expressive symbols or as truth claims, but as communally authoritative rules of discourse, attitude and action'.[37] We might feel we detect here a dangerous hint of the Wittgensteinian language game that those can play who choose to do so. Lindbeck, however, is anxious not to turn religions into 'self-enclosed and incommensurable ghettoes'.[38] In the end 'The ultimate test in this as in other areas is performance'.[39] The fact that Lindbeck regards this test as concerned with whether the theological method proves 'conceptually powerful' as well as 'practically useful' offers hope of deliverance from a simple impoverished pragmatism which, in my view, would be as unsatisfactory for theology as mere instrumentalism is for science.

However, Lindbeck is coy about the truth content to be assigned to religion. He recognizes that believers uttering such phrases as 'Jesus is Lord' and 'God is good' usually consider themselves to be speaking about what is the case. But the cases in question possess their own peculiar character, which causes discourse about them to be suitably nuanced. 'Jesus is Lord', according to Paul, can only be uttered in the Spirit (1 Corinthians 12.3). It is not just a neutral observation like 'The cat is black', but it carries the implication of commitment, with corresponding performatory consequences. 'God is good' is not equivalent to 'Jones is good', for all utterance about God concerns reference to a Being whose infinite nature so far transcends ours that all language about him must be in some stretched analogical sense.

One of the attractions of the cultural-linguistic approach for Lindbeck seems to be that it enables one to a large extent to bypass awkward questions of truth and so it is accommodating to an ecumenical view which avoids pressing points of conflict between differing traditions. In the end it seems you are encouraged to take your choice about cognitive content, for his discussion is balanced between possibilities:

> a religion can be interpreted as possibly containing ontologically true affirmations, not only in cognitivist theories but also in cultural-linguistic ones. There is nothing in the cultural-linguistic approach that requires the rejection (or the acceptance) of the epistemological realism and correspondence

theory of truth which, according to most of the theological traditions, is implicit in the conviction of believers that when they rightly use a sentence such as 'Christ is Lord' they are uttering a true first-order proposition.[40]

One is left uneasy. Why should anything be 'conceptually powerful' and 'practically useful' unless it bore some relation to the way things are? If the ultimate test is performance one could hardly imagine demanding more than is involved in the submission to martyrdom. It is difficult not to believe that the martyrs embraced their fate because they felt it to be demanded by adherence to the truth. There are two cards which, if played at all, should always be regarded as cards of last resort in rational inquiry. One is the appeal to mystery (which if used too early can simply represent succumbing to theological laziness) and the other is the abandonment of the hope of knowledge of reality (which can be a premature capitulation to agnosticism).

Lindbeck regards the propositional account of theology as being 'similar to philosophy or science as they were classically conceived'.[41] But our modern understanding of science recognizes it as being an altogether more subtle activity than an axiomatized approach would suggest, without thereby forcing the conclusion that the scientific world-view is just a paradigm socially agreed by the scientific community. There is a strongly Kuhnian flavour in Lindbeck's thought:

> Adherents of different religions do not diversely thematize the same experience, rather they have different experiences. Buddhist compassion, Christian love and... French Revolution *fraternité* are not diverse modifications of a simple human awareness, emotion, attitude or sentiment but are radically (i.e. from the root) distinct ways of experiencing and being oriented toward self, neighbour and cosmos.[42]

We do not have to accept such a claim of incommensurability, reminiscent of assertions that J. J. Thomson, Bohr and Feynman are not speaking of the same thing when they talk about an electron, because they have different detailed understandings of it. Instead we can afford a degree of 'charitable reference'[43] which allows for varying perceptions of the same root reality.[44]

Provided our concept of the rational is wide enough to comprehend the actual discourse of human reason, it is possible to adopt a position intermediate between the propositional-cognitive and cultural-linguistic views of theology. One might call it the critically realist view. In the language of Polanyi, theology will

14

be understood as being pursued in a convivial community but with universal intent. It will be both cultural and cognitive. Because of its profoundly personal character, religion will always be more culturally conditioned in its expression than is the case for science. Because of the nature of the Reality with which it has to deal, theology will always be more qualified in its attainment of even a modest degree of verisimilitude than is the case for science. Karl Barth said that the angels would laugh when they read his theology.[45] The Infinite will never be caught in nets spread out by finite minds and, in Carnes' phrase, theological statements will have to be content with the status of 'cognitive but not descriptive'.[46] Yet that cognitive status is not lightly to be abandoned.

If theology is to be found with science in the same spectrum of rational inquiry, it cannot be bracketed off as a 'normative and non-empirical discipline', as the sociologist Peter Berger describes it.[47] Admittedly theology does not offer predictions open to straightforward empirical testing such as physical science habitually does, at least at its lower levels. Partly that is because theology's understandings are framed in the broad terms of a world view (so that the sciences most akin to it are those of a historico-observational character, such as cosmology or evolutionary biology, which also do not trade in detailed predictions). Partly it is because God is not to be put to the test (Deuteronomy 6.16). Yet if theology is to maintain cognitive claims it must be an empirical discipline to the extent that its assertions are related to an understanding of experience. Theological statements unrelated to experience would be arid dogmatism; expressivist utterance not submitted to assessment and interpretation would be mere emotionalism.

As with every other specific form of inquiry, the experience considered by theology will have its own particular character, and discourse about it will need to employ its own particular modes of expression. Observer and object are linked in a mutual relationship. The nature of the object controls what can be known about it and the way in which that knowledge must be expressed. Quite the contrary to what Kant supposed, we do not impose a grid of expectation upon experience as the a priori necessity for its accessibility to us, but our manner of knowing has to be conformed to that with which we have to deal. The quantum world can be investigated and understood, but only on its own counterintuitive and unpicturable terms. A kind of version of the hermeneutic circle is involved. Analysis shows that the uncertainty principle only holds if we commit ourselves wholeheartedly to its consistent application to all phenomena. Otherwise it could be breached, as

Einstein tried to do in his long-running battle with Niels Bohr.[48]
It would be surprising indeed if the exploration of divine reality
were not subject to an analogous need to respect the nature of that
encountered.

Theology's necessary conformation to its Object has been
expressed by Torrance:

> How God can be known must be determined from first to last
> by the way in which He actually is known. It is because the
> nature of what is known, as well as the nature of the knower,
> determines how it can be known, that only when it actually is
> known are we in a position to inquire how it can be known.

He goes on to make a comparison with quantum theory and
concludes that

> all the way through theological inquiry we must operate with an
> *open* epistemology in which we allow the way of our knowing to
> be clarified and modified *pari passu* with advance in deeper and
> fuller knowledge of the object.[49]

Failure to acknowledge this is the opposite of rationality. God is
an altogether different kind of being from any finite existent and
he stands in a different relationship to his creation than does any
creature contained within it. Basil Mitchell is right to protest that
to deny God's existence 'on the sole ground that if he existed he
would constitute an exception to the manner in which we normally
provide identifying references is to beg the question against the
theist by demanding that theism accommodate itself to an essentially
atheistic metaphysic'.[50] The One who is the ground of all is bound
to be more elusive in his omnipresence than contingent beings of
whom one can say 'Lo here' or 'Lo there'. In consequence of
divine uniqueness, theological language may well be, as Ian
Ramsey said, 'object language that exhibits logical peculiarity,
logical impropriety'[51] when compared with ordinary usage. It will
be strained and stretched as the finite struggles to come to terms
with the Infinite. There will be nothing cut and dried about it, for
'theology demands and thrives on a diversity of models - theological
discourse must never be uniformly flat. Eccentricity, logical
impropriety is its very lifeblood'.[52] Even with such licence for
linguistic manoeuvre, the success of theological language will
always be strictly limited. 'The religious person must always assert
that there can be no formula guaranteed to produce God for
inspection'[53] (any more than a formula would be capable of
encapsulating human nature). Theological discourse neither despairs
of any utterance (for we are not forced to a total Wittgensteinian

silence about that which we do not know) nor does it claim privileged access to otherwise ineffable knowledge. Northrop Frye shrewdly observes that 'it is curious but significant that both "gnostic" and "agnostic" are dirty words in the Christian tradition'.[54]

After taking account of these caveats, we must press on to inquire with Ian Ramsey 'what kind of empirical anchorage have theological words?'. His answer was 'a "self awareness" which is more than "body awareness" and not exhausted by spatio-temporal "objects" '.[55] For Ramsey the quintessential experience on which theology is based is a moment of disclosure which reveals a hitherto unseen depth in what is going on. He wove a whole philosophical theology around the discussion of phrases such as 'the penny drops', 'the ice melts', indicative of such revelatory experiences.

Of course, the penny might drop in all sorts of ways that would not be reckoned religious, as when a young mathematician first grasps that $\sqrt{2}$ is not rational. Lonergan says that 'Religious conversion is being grasped by ultimate concern. It is other-worldly falling in love.'[56] There is an inescapable element of total personal involvement, so that rational theological inquiry is not a speculative investigation of what might be so but a committed response to what is found to be the case. No doubt Polanyi was right to insist on the intellectual passion involved in doing science but it pales in comparison with the openness to involvement demanded by the religious quest. Heart and mind must both be engaged for 'Commitment alone without inquiry tends to become fanaticism or narrow dogmatism; reflection alone without commitment tends to become trivial speculation unrelated to real life'.[57]

Janet Martin Soskice has suggested that there are two kinds of theologically significant experience, for the word is

> a portmanteau term to cover two sorts, the first being the dramatic or pointed religious experiences of the kind which might prompt one to say 'whatever appeared to me on the mountain was God', or 'whatever caused me to change my life was God'. The second are the different experiences which form the subject of subsequent metaphysical reflection, the kind on which Aquinas based his proofs for the existence of God.[58]

One might say that these are the encounters of revelation and the insights of natural theology, which, of course, must be capable of mutually consistent interpretation if they are indeed pointers to the one true God. The second kind of experience has a rather general character to it, whilst the first in its individuality resembles the artist's 'journey of intensification into particularity'.[59]

17

A prime context for personal encounter with God is provided by the experience of worship. Geoffrey Wainwright called Wesley's hymn book 'a little body of experimental and practical divinity'.[60] A number of recent writers have sought to frame theological discourse in terms which recognize this point of entry through worship.[61] Frequently the cultic expression of the praise of God is the trigger which brings about that moment of deeper disclosure. It was in the Temple that Isaiah had his great vision of the Lord, high and lifted up (Isaiah 6). The psalmist found there an answer to his perplexity at the prosperity of the wicked:

> But when I sought to understand this,
> it seemed to me a wearisome task,
> until I went into the sanctuary of God
> then I perceived their end.
> (Psalm 73.16-17)

Intimately connected with right worship is right conduct, for

> Who shall ascend the hill of the Lord?
> And who shall stand in his holy place?
> He that has clean hands and a pure heart.
> (Psalm 24.3-4a)

'The vision is there for the catching in the liturgy and it includes a practical component to living... Christianity yields its secret only to those who engage themselves existentially in worship and appropriate conduct.'[62] Too often theology has seemed to look to Scripture and tradition as if they were resources available for detached perusal. Of course, the written records of the foundational lives and experiences from which a religious tradition grew, and of the way in which that growth developed, are of the highest importance, but they need supplementation by what Wainwright has called the 'oral tradition' of worship. The *lex credendi* and the *lex orandi* need each other for 'The written tradition is the oral tradition's criterion of authenticity. And the oral tradition is the written tradition's interpretative guide.'[63]

Ian Ramsey liked to emphasize the logical 'oddness' of theological language 'known best in what can be called compactly "worship", a situation which is one of "discernment" and "commitment"'.[64] Here we enter a realm, not so much of universe-assisted logic, as of liturgy-assisted logic, an attempt to be 'both intellectually honest and devotionally helpful'.[65] In the act of Christian worship, Scripture and tradition (as articulated in the catholic creeds) find their proper place, maintained down the centuries by the celebration of the Eucharist where 'week by week, and month by month, on a hundred thousand successive Sundays, faithfully, unfailingly, across all the parishes of Christendom, the pastors have done just this to *make* the *plebs sancta Dei* - the holy common people of God'.[66] It is part of the structured freedom provided by the liturgy that it can accommodate within its frame the manifold individual response of the worshippers, from numinous encounter with the mystery *tremendum et fascinans*[67] to mystical incorporation into the One,[68] from the expression of trust (Psalm 27) to protest at abandonment (Psalm 38). There is a rich field on which theology can draw for the raw material for its reflection.

A defence of theology's claim to a place within the spectrum of rational inquiry into what is the case, must have an empirical aspect to it. I have sought by means of quotations from contemporary theologians to exhibit that this has been the nature of theological activity. The necessary intention to understand experience is indeed present. Consideration of great figures of the past (Augustine, Aquinas, Calvin, Schleiermacher and many others) would, in different ways, serve to confirm that theology is not ungrounded speculation but the attempt to reflect upon encounter with the divine.[69] Science and theology, for all their contrasts of subject matter and all their consequent differences of method, are indeed cousins under the skin. We shall seek to explore that affinity in the essays that follow.

2 Rational Discourse

Everyday language arises from everyday experience. The natural objects of its discourse are those entities, such as trees or chairs, about which all but the most tiresomely sceptical believe that they have direct knowledge. Chairs come in a great variety of shapes and it is not completely straightforward to define the essence of chairness (when does it become a stool?), but if all else fails we can have recourse to ostensive definition and exhibit sufficient examples to induce intuition about what is involved. Yet we habitually speak also of entities which are not directly observable. No one has ever seen a gene (though there are X-ray photographs which, suitably interpreted, led Crick and Watson to the helical structure of DNA) or an electron (though there are tracks in bubble chambers which, suitably interpreted, indicate the presence of a particle of negative electric charge of about $4.8 \cdot 10^{-10}$ esu and mass about 10^{-27} gm). No one has ever seen God (though there is the astonishing Christian claim that 'the only Son, who is in the bosom of the Father, he has made him known' (John 1.18)).

Entities which are not ostensible will have to be referred to allusively; what is unfamiliar will have to be described by means of some form of analogy with the familiar. As our examples indicate, this problem of discourse is one which science and theology share. Both have to trade in model and metaphor. We have to inquire the extent to which their experiences might prove mutually illuminating. Such exploration rapidly leads one into a semantic minefield, full of danger for the unwary traveller who will be offered many incompatible definitions of what purport to be the same term. It is best to start the journey in a part of the terrain with which one is reasonably familiar. Consequently I shall begin with science.

My examples will be chosen from contemporary physics. Although this will not be a scene altogether familiar to every reader, our concern will only be with certain general aspects of method. These can be made accessible to those prepared to trust the author not to distort the story and who are content not to demand an itemized account of every detail. Modern physical theory exhibits sophisticated patterns of development which should be taken into account in serious discussion. We ought not to condemn ourselves to endless reconsideration of instructive but limited cases drawn from nineteenth-century physics, such as that old war horse of this kind of engagement, the kinetic theory of gases.

It seems to me that the word 'model' is used scientifically in a quite consistent sense, to mean a frankly heuristic device by which one attempts to gain some purchase on reality or some insight into complexity, without believing that one is giving a totally accurate account of that reality or a fully adequate characterization of that complexity. A model is potentially illuminating but not exhaustively descriptive. Let me give some examples.

Investigations into the structure of matter[1] suggested that nucleons and their excited states (resonances) should be thought of as if they were composed of fractionally charged constituents (quarks) which, when struck by high energy projectiles, behaved as if they were freely moving within the particle in question but which, nevertheless, were confined, that is to say, they could not escape from the particle however violent the impact. This insight could be stated in terms of what was called the Quark Parton Model (QPM). This model could be formulated with varying degrees of sophistication, but all had a certain *ad hoc* character. They assumed a 'softness' condition which gave the freely moving behaviour and they stipulated confinement as an interpretative principle, imposed in defiance of a more natural understanding which would have described a recoiling quark, visible in the laboratory. No one could suppose so contrived a scheme to be a fully satisfactory account of the structure of matter. QPM was not a case of 'telling it like it is', but it was a theoretical tool which proved very successful in exploring certain aspects of high energy physics. In a particular physical regime (deep inelastic scattering) it explained a behaviour (scaling) which proved to be the case to a high degree of approximation. QPM enabled one to correlate deep inelastic scattering experiments using different projectiles and target particles in ways which were naturally interpreted as manifesting the quark property of fractional charge. The model could also be used in certain other physical regimes (technically: $e^+ e^-$ annihilation; Drell-Yan production of lepton pairs), where it proved capable of making useful and successful predictions.

There were some questions, however, which QPM could not address. One was the nature of the hadronic spectrum, that is to say, what were the masses and other properties of the resonances made out of quarks? To attempt to get some sort of grip on these phenomena, a different model was invented. It too was of a frankly heuristic character. It pictured the particles as being containers with rigid walls, confining the freely moving quarks within them. This Bag Model (to give it its technical name) was quite tricky to set up, because it had to be done in a relativistic fashion, which is

21

not easy to achieve with rigid boundaries. When this had been solved, the model proved modestly successful in helping to understand a limited but significant range of phenomena, different from those covered by QPM. No one believed for a moment that hadrons were actually bags of quarks in that simplistic sense, but it was a fruitful approach to take, provided you used it with appropriate caution.

At much the same time that all this was going on, elementary particle physicists were playing with another kind of model which had arisen from considering yet another set of phenomena. It is harder than QPM or the Bag Model to describe in nonprofessional language (for the technically informed, I am referring to the Veneziano model of duality). Let me content myself by saying that there was a suspicion that results which might have been expected to arise from the combination of two distinct causes, were in fact due to a single cause incorporating both sets of effects in a most surprising way. Here the question was whether such a subtle combination was indeed a consistent possibility. Gabriele Veneziano produced a brilliantly simple model which did the trick of two-for-the-price-of-one for all to see. Once again, certain crude simplifications meant that the Veneziano model could not be taken literally as a description of reality, but it was an extremely instructive source of insight.

I think that these stories are typical of the use of models in physics. Each model seeks to reproduce certain gross features of physical reality, selected because they are believed to be the ones of greatest importance for understanding a specific regime. One might think of a model as being a coarse-grained representation, applicable in a limited domain. In some cases it may prove useful outside the regime for which it was originally constructed, as when QPM gave insight into lepton pair production, but no one expects it to have a universal validity. In consequence, the existence of differing models (QPM and Bags) in disjoint regimes causes no difficulty or astonishment. Veneziano's work is an interesting example of the use of a model to explore the consistency of a novel hypothesis. I think this latter use may have been at least part of what lay behind Lord Kelvin's celebrated assertion 'I never satisfy myself until I can make a mechanical model of a thing'.[2] We do not have to suppose Kelvin to have been caught in the grip of a narrow-minded adherence to mechanism, but we may simply credit him with a desire to understand the possibility of the unfamiliar by reference to the familiar. The fantastic ingenuity of the wheels-within-wheels models of the aether, constructed by nineteenth-century physicists, can be seen as attempts to probe the consistency of assuming the existence of a subtle medium with remarkable properties. One can hardly suppose them to have been invented as candidate descriptions of the structure of space.

This view of models as heuristic devices, shorn of ontological pretensions but valuable for a crude ability to represent the structure critical in certain circumstances, is echoed by a number of writers. Lonergan said of models that they 'purport to be, not descriptions of reality, not hypotheses about reality, but simply interlocking sets of terms and relations... useful in guiding investigations, in framing hypotheses and in uniting descriptions'.[3] Barbour calls a model 'an imaginative tool, for ordering experience, rather than a description of the world';[4] they are to be taken 'seriously but not literally'.[5] Peacocke states that 'Models in both science and theology are concerned less with picturing objects than with depicting processes, relations and structures (i.e. patterns of relationships)'.[6] Less happy, because lacking the focus on a limited but specific intent to discover, is Soskice's wide-ranging definition that 'an object or state of affairs is said to be a model when it is viewed in terms of some other object or state of affairs'.[7]

Models, as I construe the term, are valuable but of recognized inadequacy. They are aids to understanding, but their successful construction is not the end of the scientific search. What is really desired is not a portfolio of models but a single theory. I will define a theory as a candidate for the verisimilitudinous description of physical reality throughout a widely prescribed domain. Our expectation is limited to verisimilitude because we do not have reason to anticipate absolute success. The attainment of an all-embracing account of phenomena for all systems of certain size and circumstance (for instance, down to 10^{-15} cm and below 1000 Gev in energy) is the best that we can hope for - a map representing all features on a given scale but ignorant of smaller detail. Because a theory, within its own domain, aims at comprehensiveness, it is only tolerable to believe in one such theory at a time. Models, on the other hand, can be accepted in plurality, for each will only find utility in its own particular set of conditions.

Study of the quark theory of matter eventually yielded a theory, quantum chromodynamics (QCD). Technically, it is a gauge field theory describing the interactions of quarks and gluons. Details do not concern us here; we simply note that QCD is currently accepted by elementary particle physicists as the preferred account of the nature of matter at this level. To write down the equations of such a theory is one thing; to establish their consequences is quite another. Some progress can be made by theoretical probing. In the case of QCD a technique called the renormalization group enabled one to elicit a scaling type of behaviour in deep inelastic scattering, which proved to be slightly modified from that given by QPM, in a direction giving even better agreement with experiment. Other problems, such as that of the hadronic spectrum, did not yield to theoretical analysis. In that case, recourse had to be made once again to the use of a model, but its coarse-grained representation could now be based on what were expected to be the relevant structural details of the theory itself, rather than on a merely phenomenological picture of particles made up of quarks. The Bag Model calculations gave way to lattice gauge theory, a simplified version of QCD in which the spacetime continuum is replaced by a network of discrete points. The latter's literal coarseness of grain is held to be an acceptable approximation, greatly assisting attempts at computation.

QCD does not accommodate the property of duality discussed by Veneziano. However there is a hotly discussed theory of superstrings which would both contain duality and have QCD as a 'low energy' limit. The quotation marks around 'low energy' are necessary because what is here meant is what is, in fact, high energy in terms of contemporary experiments, but which is many orders of magnitude smaller than the characteristic energies associated with strings of length 10^{-33} cm. Such a notion is highly speculative but if it were to prove to be the case it would exemplify the sort of nesting relationship we have come to expect between theories operating in different domains of physics. The larger-scale theories (classical physics in relation to quantum physics, QCD in relation to superstrings) are reconciled with the finer-grained theories by the former describing behaviour of the latter in appropriate limiting circumstances. This 'correspondence principle' relationship is essential to the claim of science to preserve a convergent verisimilitude despite occasional substantial changes in the character of basic physical theory.

Desirable as the possession of a theory undoubtedly is, it would often be incapable of yielding extensive explanatory power without recourse to the use of models for its exploitation. As one moves from the simplicities of elementary particle physics to the complications inherent in larger aggregations of matter, this becomes only too clear. Consider the case of theoretical chemistry. No one could doubt that the basic force responsible (electromagnetism) and the basic dynamical theory (quantum mechanics) are well known. The necessary equations (those associated with the names of Maxwell and Schrödinger) can indeed be written comfortably on a T-shirt. Yet eliciting their consequences for a particular molecular structure is far from being a straightforward corollary.

Theoretical chemists construct a variety of models of chemical bonding in the effort to get a purchase, in different circumstances, on the actual nature of valency. The variety of these models, and their mutual incompatibilities if construed too literally, in no way detract from the rational character of theoretical chemistry nor deny the possession of an underlying theory correctly accepted by all. They simply testify to the difficulty of the detailed task.

Sometimes in science, what had been thought of as a theory turns out to be no more than a model. One of the very greatest achievements of nineteenth-century physics was Maxwell's electromagnetic wave theory of light. Yet the early years of this century saw the recognition that this was only half the story. In certain situations, typically diffraction experiments, waves are indeed the way to think, but in other circumstances, such as the photoelectric effect, an entirely different particle model is needed to make sense of what is going on. Scientists could not rest content with so bitty an account and it was a great relief when in 1927 Paul Dirac invented quantum field theory, which truly qualifies for the status of a theory by its ability to contain both the wave and particle aspects of light without inconsistency.[8]

Wave-and-particle is an example of a complementary pair of models, apparently contradictory but saved from disaster by being applicable in mutually exclusive circumstances. This is a feature of quantum mechanics to which Niels Bohr drew particular attention.[9] Complementarity is deeply embedded in quantum theory, extending to the formalism itself, which can be expressed either in position terms (configuration space) or in terms of momentum (momentum space). Each formulation says all that can be said about the system and we have a free choice of which approach to use, though obviously one or the other may be better suited to a particular situation. This kind of complementarity seems more profound than just the coexistence of different models usable in different domains, for it says that the whole of what is going on can be read in a position-like or a momentum-like way, even if one or the other might be pretty inconvenient for a specific purpose.

Bohr felt that the notion of complementarity constituted a very general interpretative principle which could be applied to many realms of thought outside physics. Let me sound a note of caution. Complementarity does not offer us an effortless means of reconciling the irreconcilable, of living with as many unresolved paradoxes as take our fancy. In quantum theory we are able to understand what is going on. Wave and particle are accommodated within quantum field theory without a taint of paradox; the general transformation theory of quantum mechanics explains how

25

configuration-space and momentum-space descriptions relate to each other. Other rational forms of inquiry are more difficult to pursue than physics, so it may well be that if complementarity has a role in them we shall not be so wholly successful in understanding how it works. A search for some glimmer of understanding is nevertheless an essential part of the intellectual quest if complementarity is to be more than a slogan.

Donald MacKay suggested that complementarity provided a way of thinking about the mutual relationship of the religious and the scientific views of the world.[10] He acknowledged the danger of attempting too facile a reconciliation:

> How can you distinguish between two pictures that are genuinely complementary, and two which are really incompatible rivals? A fair question, indeed. When *are* we justified in insisting that two pictures must be complementary? The answer I think must be: Only when we find both are necessary to do justice to experience.[11]

It is the typical answer of the physicist: we accept what reality forces upon us, putting our faith in the ultimate rationality of the world. There is a lot to be said for such an approach, not least because of its openness to what goes beyond the confining limits of our prior expectation. The careful analyses of the philosophers would have been unlikely to do more than articulate somewhat laboriously the common-sense apprehension that wave and particle are very different kinds of entities. The search for their reconciliation in quantum field theory only came about under the pressure of circumstance, pointing to the need for such an 'impossible' combination. It was an act of universe-assisted logic.

Ian Barbour takes a more critical view of using complementarity. He says of science and religion:

> They do not refer to the same entity. They arise typically in differing situations and serve differing functions in human life. For these reasons I will speak of science and religion as alternative languages, and restrict the term 'complementary' to models of the same logical type *within* a given language.[12]

He will not go further than using complementarity to refer to different accounts (numinous/mystical; personal/impersonal God) within a single religious tradition.

Barbour exaggerates the degree of separation between the phenomena of science and religion. In the broadest sense, both explore aspects of the one world encountered in our experience. Moreover, there are clearly areas in which their concerns overlap.

The physicist's account of cosmic process and the theologian's doctrine of God's continuing act of creation are viewing – to be sure from different perspectives – the same object (the cosmos). The questions they address are certainly not the same, and the answers given are of contrasting kinds,[13] but at the very least there must be some degree of consonance between them. The fact that the universe we experience today has evolved over fifteen billion years from an initial state of great simplicity, rather than having sprung into being ready-made a few thousand years ago, has certainly had its effect on the tone of theological discourse. If the 'language' being spoken is that of rational discourse, then both science and theology operate within it. Possibly MacKay exaggerates the value of having a name for what is often a perplexity. Complementarity is not by itself an instantly explanatory concept. It is simply suggestive of a search for understanding which seeks to take an even-handed view of two accounts of what is going on. Natural theology pursues just such a reconcilement of science and religion, even if its proponents have not been as successful in the task as Dirac was with the invention of quantum field theory.

The appeal of some form of complementary-style understanding is even greater when we consider the most significant area in which science and theology impinge upon each other, namely in their accounts of what it is to be human. MacKay, with his professional concern for brain science, frequently discussed in these terms the question of how what he called the I-story (the internal account of personal experience) and the O-story (the external account given by an observer) relate to each other. Elsewhere I have suggested that it might be possible to approach the age-old problem of mind and brain, neither along the lines of the exclusivist accounts of materialism or idealism, nor along the line of the unresolved duality of Cartesianism, but following a complementary metaphysic, sketched in rudimentary terms as the notion that human participation in a noetic world arises from mind being the complementary pole to matter in flexible open organization.[14]

It is clear that theology employs a multitude of models in its attempt to discourse of God. He can be pictured as a Stern Judge or a Loving Father. The tension between these two accounts occasions no surprise, for they will be applicable in different situations. The former may be the prelude to repentance, the latter may be the consequence of the experience of sins forgiven – Luther before and after his wrestling with the Epistle to the Romans, if one wants a concrete example. God has not changed his nature but the encounter with him has altered its mode. Ian Barbour, following some suggestions of Tillich, proposes that we should recognize the utility of both personal and impersonal models of divinity.[15] The one may be fitting for expressing the experiences of revelation, the other for expressing the insights of natural theology. In that way Christian theology can submit to the necessity of which F. R. Tennant spoke when he said that it 'must be sufficiently tinged with deism to recognize a relatively settled order'.[16] We do not have to choose between the dangerously anthropomorphic God of the Bible and the dangerously remote God of the philosophers, for both are models of aspects of the complexity of the divine nature.

Theology needs no reminder of the ontological inadequacy and limited utility of any particular model. The prohibitions of idolatry and the warnings of apophatic theology against rational overconfidence are directed to these very points. After elaborating his theological system, Thomas Aquinas had a profound spiritual experience of the presence of God which caused him to speak of his intellectual labours as being no more than 'straw'. Perhaps the brilliant edifice of the *Summa Theologiae* is the nearest theology has ever come to the construction of a theory, but that will never prove wholly possible for a discipline whose Object transcends us, in contrast to science's object, the physical world, which we transcend. To acknowledge this is not to despair of any prospect of rational inquiry in theology, but simply to be appropriately realistic about what its character will be. It will employ many models but it will always fall short of a fully articulated theory. While an all-embracing coherence may elude theology, and paradoxes may prove unavoidable, needless indulgence in mystery is to be avoided. The theologian remains alert to the necessity for the greatest attainable degree of coherence. The long Christian discussion of how the Old and New Testaments relate to each other is reminiscent of the search for correspondence principles reconciling the new insights of Einstein with the old insights of Newton. The 'Kuhnian' view expressed by Marcion, that the two Testaments were incommensurable paradigms, was firmly rejected.

The models employed by physical science are essentially mathematical in character. Even an apparently picturable model, like the kinetic theory's view of a gas as a collection of colliding billiard balls, or the wave picture of light, depends for its calculational power upon expression in a mathematical form. *A fortiori* that is true of physical *theory*. The fact that successful theory is not only mathematical, but also has about it the unmistakable character of mathematical beauty, is a profoundly significant fact about the world. In my view, it finds coherent explanation in terms of natural theology.[17] It is important to recognize that this deep role for mathematics goes far beyond a simple need to cope with the quantitative. What is involved is not mere numeration but the structure-analysing, pattern-creating power of abstract mathematics. It is difficult to illustrate this for the non-mathematical reader, but gauge field theories in elementary particle physics and Riemannian geometry in cosmology have precisely this character. The contemporary speculative study of superstrings has been encouraged by their apparent potential for structural elegance. Because I believe mathematics to be the natural language for the formulation of physical theory, I do not make the distinction, insisted upon by Barbour,[18] between mathematical and theoretical models. To say this is not in the least to equate theoretical physics with pure mathematics, because an indispensable element in a model or theory in theoretical physics is the set of interpretative rules by which the mathematical formalism is put in correspondence with observable phenomena. It is to assert, however, that (with partial adequacy in a model and verisimilitude in a theory) there is an isomorphism (corresponding identity of structure) between mathematical patterns and physical patterns, which makes the former explanatory of the latter.

What then do we make of the role of metaphor in scientific discourse? Janet Martin Soskice says:

> Only someone completely unacquainted with the language of the natural sciences could believe that it contains no metaphors at all; even the most uninformed has run across phrases such as 'time warp', 'particle charm' or 'black hole', whose use he realizes to be figurative, although he may not be certain what they signify.[19]

The question needs closer attention. Some of these phrases serve as suggestive shorthand for the properly articulatable concepts lying behind them (such as the geometrical configuration of space-time corresponding to a black hole singularity). As Soskice acknowledges, the particular phrase has then simply a subsidiary role in conveying to a non-scientist some kind of a notion of what would otherwise be inaccessible. It is by way of popularization, rather than scientific discourse itself, that their use is metaphorical. Other phrases, such as 'charm', are just picturesque terms introduced to give a certain lightness to what would otherwise be an unrelieved technical discussion. Their dispensability is made clear by the fact that they can be employed correctly as ciphers, without their being interpreted in accordance with their originator's intention. In common with many elementary particle physicists I had long believed that 'charm' was a facetious

29

appellation used in the sense of 'delight'. I was surprised to learn recently that it was invented with the sense of 'amulet' in mind, because the existence of the charm quantum number provides a way of warding off the evil of an unobserved experimental consequence which would otherwise be present in the theory.[20] This misapprehension in no way spoiled my understanding of the physics involved.

I do not doubt, however, that there is some degree of metaphorical usage in physics. It depends upon exploiting intuitive understanding of a range of well-studied phenomena, held to bear an analogical relation to the new phenomena under consideration. For example, there is a model for the behaviour of large nuclei which goes by the name of the 'liquid drop' model. Those equipped with an understanding of how fluid drops divide, were able to comprehend, without detailed calculations, certain features of the fission of heavy nuclei.

Usage of this kind hovers on the brink of the truly metaphorical. It has more of the plain comparison of the simile to it, than that openness of reference which seems to characterize the metaphor. Soskice defines metaphor's place among the tropes as being 'that figure of speech by which we speak about one thing in terms which seem suggestive of another'.[21] There is, of course, a good deal more to metaphor than just that, which it is one of the purposes of her book to explore. Metaphor is not to be pinned down. There is something both elusive and allusive about it which yields a creative flexibility, essential for the discussion of those realms of experience which cannot be dispassionately objectified. A critical realism in the personal domain calls for appropriate use of metaphor, since here we need terms whose 'lack of strict definitional stipulation . . . *allows* for the revisability necessary to any account that aims to adapt itself to the world'.[22] The personal is the interactive and 'As we think of words it is only metaphor that can express in language the sense of energy common to subject and object'.[23] Nothing else will do in certain unfamiliar realms for 'metaphor is a strategy of desperation, not decoration; it is an attempt to say something about the unfamiliar in terms of the familiar, an attempt to speak about what we do not know in terms of what we do know'.[24] Metaphor can carry us into regimes of thought which would otherwise be inaccessible. 'Whether we speak of the metaphorical character of metaphysics or the metaphysical character of metaphor, what must be grasped is the single movement that carries things beyond, *meta*'.[25]

We think of Austin Farrer's remark about poetry: 'The phrase which is just right has infinite overtones; or it awakens echoes in the hidden caves of our minds'.[26] There is something irreducible about poetry. Like jokes, it can never quite submit itself to translation. Metaphor is the poet's indispensable way of expressing what is on the edge of inexpressibility, his 'chief test and glory'.[27] Theology faces an even more daunting task as it attempts to speak of the Ineffable. 'The great divine and the great poet have this in common: both use metaphor to say what can be said in no other way but which, once said, can be recognized by many'.[28] Here is exhibited the greatest skill, to say what had been thought to be beyond the telling. The literary critic, Northrop Frye, said of the Bible that it 'belongs to an area of language where metaphor is functional, and where we have to surrender precision to flexibility'.[29] To say that is not to invoke a cloudy licence but simply to recognize that discourse must be shaped by the nature of that about which it seeks to speak. The attempt to pin down the Infinite to precise finite expression is the sin of idolatry.

If mathematics is the natural language of physical science, symbol is the natural language of theology. A symbol is the most intense form of metaphor. Sally McFague speaks of it as being the 'sedimentation and solidification of metaphor',[30] but a more appropriate image might be that of apotheosis, for the symbol can be seen as possessing a vitality of its own. Ricoeur said 'the symbol gives: I do not posit the meaning, the symbol gives it',[31] and the thought reminds us of how Farrer spoke of those living images which he said were 'the stuff of inspiration':

> The various images are not, of course, unconnected in the Apostle's [Paul's] mind, they attract one another and tend to fuse, but they have their own way of doing this, according to their own imagery laws, and not according to the principles of conceptual system.[32]

In the gap between the signifier and the signified, symbols possess room for manoeuvre which affords them the power to carry the 'surplus meaning' about which Paul Ricoeur spoke so much. Herein lies the crucial distinction between a symbol and a sign. The latter is just a substitutable cipher, possessing no more than the force of convention. It is capable of being perceived in the same way by many different people. The symbol carries a cloud of allusion and suggestion which enables individuals to respond to it in their own way. When someone wears a Union Flag on his anorak, it is simply a sign that he is British. When the Union Flag is carried as the Queen's Colour on the anniversary of a regimental battle honour, it possesses the symbolic power to invoke the glory and ambiguity of past history and to invite a present participation.

'Only a symbol? He who asks this question shows that he has not understood the difference between signs and symbols nor the power of symbolic language'.[33] Of course, there is nothing automatic in the operation of a symbol. It can degenerate into a sign or be perverted into an idol. Ricoeur said that 'symbols give rise to thought' but 'they are also the birth of idols. That is why the critique of idols remains the condition of the conquest of symbols'.[34]

If this characterization of symbol is correct, and I am persuaded that it is,[35] it becomes intelligible why it should provide the natural language of theology. Symbol, like sacrament, is neither to be reified (a temptation for catholic theology) nor reduced to a mere sign (a temptation for reformed theology) but 'It participates in the power of what it symbolizes, and therefore can be a medium of the Spirit'.[36] Karl Rahner said of theology that it 'is incomprehensible if it is not a theology of symbols'. The symbol 'is itself full of the thing it symbolizes, being its concrete form of existence'.[37] Rahner defines a symbol as 'the representation which allows the other "to be there"'.[38] The language is deliberately sacramental in tone and reminds us that symbols are not only verbal. I have suggested that the experience of worship is central to theology (see Chapter 1), and central to Christian worship are the symbols of the bread and wine of the Eucharist. To say so is not to adopt a Zwinglian reductionist manner of speaking but to share in what Dillistone says is Rahner's belief that 'A real symbol constitutes a real presence'.[39]

A particular kind of symbol is provided by those stories carrying an open and profound significance which leads us to classify them as myths. The continuing power of the primeval history of Genesis 1-11 and of the *Iliad* and the *Odyssey* testify to the force of this kind of symbolic tale. David Brown speaks of myth as being a 'concept where meaning outruns form'.[40] Myths seem to have an indispensable role in human thought. Tillich says of them that 'One can replace one myth by another, but one cannot remove the myth from man's spiritual life'.[41] Perhaps nothing makes that clearer than the way in which modern science has been used to provide replacement myths for those unable to use the traditional stories of religion. While scientific discourse itself does not employ the mythic mode, its accounts, particularly those dealing with the history and process of the cosmos, have furnished material that can be used in this way. The rhetorical and moving defiance in the face of a universe perceived to be meaningless, articulated by Jacques Monod in *Chance and Necessity*,[42] is based on the myth of an empire of accident, a world in which chance reigns supreme.

(I have suggested elsewhere that one does not need to read the scientific story that way.[43]) Much of the public interest in cosmology, and much of the popular writing ministering to it, carry overtones of mythic concern. Even extreme reductionism can become the basis of a myth.[44]

Many would claim that myths are useful fictions, rafts to float on seas too deep for other forms of knowledge. Alasdair MacIntyre says that 'A myth is living or dead, not true or false'.[45] Here is a seductive opportunity to retain the power of biblical narrative without embarrassment to a modern scientific world view. What is required, according to this approach, is not demythologization but deliteralization. It is clear enough that we have to go some way down that path. A belief in an historic Adam and Eve and serpent is surely not required. Yet when Carnes says 'if we can say, in some accepted sense, that the *Antigone* is "true", then it may not seem strange to say *in the same sense*, the Christian story is true',[46] I become very uneasy. While there is power in symbolic story, there is a different power in a story of what has actually happened. I believe the two powers are marvellously combined in the Christian story of the incarnation:

> The power of myth and the power of actuality fuse in the incarnation. What could be more profound than that God should take human form, make himself known in human terms, share the suffering of the strange world he has made and on the cross open his arms to embrace its bitterness? Yet it is no tale projected on to a shadowy figure of ancient legend. It is concerned with what actually happened in the concrete person of Jesus Christ, a wandering teacher in a particular province of the Roman Empire, at a particular point in history. The centre of Christianity lies in the *realized myth* of the incarnation.[47]

I do not think that we have to rest content with a metaphorical theology which, in Sally McFague's words, is '*mostly* fiction' – which 'although it "says much", it "means little"'.[48]

The word symbol comes from the Greek *symbollein*, to bring together. The Christian understanding of Jesus is as the true Symbol, bearing the stamp of the divine nature (Hebrews 1.3), in whom are brought together revelation and reconciliation, the human and the divine.

3 The Nature of Physical Reality

'There is no sense in which subatomic particles are to be graded as "more real" than, say, a bacterial cell or a human person, or even social facts.'[1] The words are those of that resolute antireductionist, Arthur Peacocke. In a series of writings he has defended the existence of level autonomy in our descriptions of the physical world. Biology has its own concepts and understandings which are not reducible to complicated corollaries of physics and chemistry.[2] I certainly agree that this is so.[3] Yet it is hard indeed to dispel altogether from one's thinking a certain reductionist tendency. When we start to consider the nature of physical reality it is instinctive to turn first to the insights of so-called fundamental science, to start with elementary particle physics and its spatially big brother, cosmology. Our discussion then becomes one of 'emergence': how, within physics itself and beyond it, new properties arise – such as the power of 'classical measuring apparatus' to determine the outcome of uncertain quantum mechanical experiments; the ability of complex molecules to replicate themselves; the coming to be of consciousness, self-consciousness, worship. In actual fact, we understand very little of how these different levels relate to each other. The problems are mostly too hard for current knowledge, despite the stunning successes of molecular biology in casting light on the physical basis of genetics. But the direction in which to look for an understanding seems clear enough. It will come from being able to relate the higher level to the lower. Emergence is conceived as a one-way process, by which the higher whole arises from the complex organization of its lower parts.

The reasons for thinking this way appear clear enough. Vitalism seems dead and even the most fervent antireductionist in relation to concepts accepts a structural reductionism. Physical reality is made out of the entities described by fundamental physics – quarks and gluons and electrons (or superstrings, or whatever). Hence the feeling that if one day we wrote the equations of a Theory of Everything on our T-shirts, then we should have got somewhere, despite the fact that in terms of our actual understanding of the physical world those equations would be more like the precise statement of the problem, rather than its solution. Another encouragement to such a bottom–up way of thinking is that it recapitulates the way in which we believe the actual complexity of being to have come about. First there was the quark soup of the primeval universe; then nuclear matter after those famous first three minutes;[4] then simple atoms when the background radiation was 'frozen' out after about half a million years; much later the complex molecules in the shallow seas of early Earth; then unicellular life; then animals; then *homo sapiens*. 'Ontogeny recapitulates phylogeny', not only embryologically but also conceptually.

Yet it is possible that if subatomic particles are not 'more real' than cells or persons, then they are not more fundamental either. It is possible that emergence is, in fact, a two-way process; that it would be conceptually valid and valuable to attempt to traverse the ladder of complexity in both directions, not only relating the higher to the lower but also the lower to the higher. Such a proposal goes somewhat beyond the mere acknowledgement of level autonomy, for it suggests the existence of a degree of reciprocity between levels.

I am tempted to explore this notion because of a recent development in physics itself. I refer to that theory of complex dynamical systems which goes under the not altogether appropriate name of the theory of chaos.[5] It provides a perfect example of the fallacy of the 'T-shirt' approach to understanding the world. Consider, for instance, the following simple equation relating a quantity x_{n+1} to its predecessor in the sequence, x_n:

$$x_{n+1} = k.x_n \left(1 - x_n\right) \quad (1)$$

The equation arises quite naturally in biological contexts, where the x's can be population sizes in successive years. Next year's population (x_{n+1}) depends upon how many of the species there are to breed this year (x_n) and on a factor which represents the attenuating effect of competition for limited resources if the population gets too big (here this factor is $(1 - x_n)$, where the variable x is a scaled population size chosen to make the equation look simple).[6] The proportionality factor k is a measure of how strong the coupling of the population is in one year to the combination of these two effects in the previous season. It is a parameter controlling possible growth rate.

If k is too small (less than 1), then x tends to zero with increasing n. The population is insufficiently fertile to maintain itself and it dies out after a few years. We are dealing with an endangered species. Past that danger level, one might expect that the population for a given value of k would maintain itself at an eventually stable level, finely tuned to the available resources. For some values of k that is indeed the case. For example, if $k = 2$, the population may fluctuate for a few years but it soon settles down to a steady $x = 0.5$. (Try it on a calculator, choosing some value of x at which to begin and seeing how quickly it homes in, after repetitions of the formula, to the value $1/2$.) However, beyond $k = 3$ that is no longer the case. For example at $k = 3.2$ one finds that the population oscillates between two values; good and bad years alternate. That also is intuitively understandable, but the plot thickens after that. Once one gets above $k = 3.5$, the cycles rapidly complicate. First there is a fourfold cycle, then an eightfold, then sixteenfold,... By the time you get to about $k = 3.58$ the population just jigs around in a completely random fashion and no stable repeating pattern is ever established. We have entered the region of behaviour which is called chaotic.

What is the moral of this mathematical tale? It is this: a simple and *perfectly deterministic* equation can produce behaviour which is random to the point of unpredictability. The latter statement demands explanation. When k is in the region corresponding to chaos, the behaviour of x is immensely sensitive to the choice of starting value. Suppose one compares calculations starting with $x = 0.3$ and with $x = 0.3001$, initial conditions which differ by less than one part in a thousand. For a few repetitions of the calculation they will keep roughly in step but quite soon the calculations will diverge from each other, giving totally different behaviours. It is characteristic of chaotic systems generally that unless one knows the initial circumstances with *unlimited* accuracy, one can only project their behaviour a small way into the future with any confidence. Beyond that they are intrinsically unpredictable.

It will not surprise you to learn that this feature of chaotic unpredictability first came to light during computer investigations of weather forecasting, using simple models of the behaviour of the atmosphere. It gives rise to 'what is only half-jokingly known as the Butterfly Effect – the notion that a butterfly stirring the air today in Peking can transform storm systems next month in New York'.[7] Yet there is also a contained randomness about the behaviour of chaotic systems. They do not wander all over the place but their motions home in on the continual and haphazard exploration of a limited range of possibilities (called a strange attractor). There is an orderly disorder in their behaviour. That is why chaos theory was not a well-chosen name.

Similarly there is a structure to the onset of chaos. Our discussion of equation (1) showed a cascading explosion of bifurcations taking place: a twofold cycle branched to give a fourfold cycle, which branched to give an eightfold cycle, and so on – each branching following yet more rapidly on its predecessor. It was a capital discovery by Mitchell Feigenbaum that this behaviour has a universal character. The precise way in which it happens is not a special property of equation (1) but it is the same for all systems which become chaotic in this bifurcating fashion.[8] Here we see not only the emergence of order from chaos but also the emergence of universality from particularity. This is both a gain and a loss. One reaches widely applicable conclusions, but at the cost of losing power to probe the nature of the underlying mechanism. Ian Stewart comments that 'Feigenbaum's discovery of universality is a two-edged sword. It makes it relatively easy to test a particular class of chaotic models; but it doesn't distinguish between the different models in that class'.[9]

A structure in which branches divide into sub-branches, and so on for ever, is an example of what the mathematicians call a fractal. Fractals are entities which look the same on whatever scale you examine them. Trees are approximately fractal. The way the trunk divides into limbs is very similar to the way the limbs divide into branches, which is very similar to the way the branches divide into twigs. Whether you look at the whole tree, or the twigs of a branch, the patterns are at least roughly the same. The most complicated entity known to the mathematicians is also approximately fractal. It is called the Mandelbrot set, after the Frenchman who first realized its astonishing fecundity. Its definition is comparatively simple to state mathematically;[10] its structure is inexhaustibly rich – whorls and dragons' claws made out of whorls and dragons' claws. Coloured computer simulations of parts of the set are fascinatingly beautiful.[11] They have become favourite subjects for the covers of scientific books. There is enough to go round for everyone who wants to publish, since you have only to blow up part of an old pattern to reveal a new pattern, approximately similar but subtly different.

The general picture resulting from these considerations is that of deterministic equations giving rise to random behaviour; of order and disorder interlacing each other; of unlimited complexity being generated by simple specification; of precise equations having unpredictable consequences. That there are these possibilities is very surprising to those of us who were brought up on the study of those 'tame', predictable mathematical systems on which we cut our mathematical teeth and which provided the standard teaching examples for generations of students. The recognition of structured chaos has been hailed as a third revolution, worthy to be set alongside the Newtonian and quantum mechanical revolutions which preceded it.[12]

The resulting world view is certainly not that of a dull mechanical regularity. Indeed, the behaviour envisaged has more than a touch of the organismic about it. This feeling is reinforced by consideration of other insights into physical process that have been gained in recent years. I am thinking of the study of dissipative systems, whose behaviour has been a major topic for investigation by Ilya Prigogine and his collaborators.[13] These systems are maintained far from equilibrium by an inflow of energy from the environment. The spontaneous triggering effects of small fluctuations, too tiny to be directly discernible, induce an order which is maintained by the flow of energy. The red spot of Jupiter, which has maintained its shape for centuries amidst the turbulent eddies of that planet's atmosphere, is thought to be an example. The order thus supported may be dynamically changing, as in the case of the so-called chemical clock. With a carefully controlled steady inflow and outflow of materials, the chemical constituents present in a mixture are found in certain circumstances to perform rhythmic oscillations from one concentration to another and back again, an astonishing effect involving the 'collaboration' of trillions of molecules. In this kind of phenomenon one sees the generation of novel and large-scale order which seems quite incomprehensible at the microscopic molecular level. Physics is found to describe processes endowed not just with being but also with becoming.

The physical systems about which I have been talking are complicated, but they fall far short of the complexity of even the simplest living cell. Its biochemical dance also exhibits the combination of openness and order which we have encountered. In an as yet small and imperfect way, one might hope to begin to see some chance of gaining modest insight into how the levels of physics and biology might eventually be found to interlock in their description of the world. Prigogine and Stengers say of their account of these matters that 'we can see ourselves as part of the universe we describe'.[14]

Wonderful! But is it all an illusion? How really open are chaotic systems? Certainly, they are unpredictable, but that is because of the inexactitude of our knowledge of initial conditions, combined with these systems' exquisite sensitivity to the precise character of those conditions. Yet the examples we have considered are all, in fact, deterministic. Take equation (1) in the chaotic regime. If I really knew that I started with $x = 0.3$ (and not, say, 0.3000001) then all the subsequent x's are explicitly calculable from the formula, however they may jig around. In other words, what we have encountered so far is no more than an epistemological limitation (our inability to know enough detail to determine what will happen) without its having any real ontological consequence (what is actually the case is still fully determined in its outcome). That is certainly so for equation (1). Is it also true for more complex and physically interesting systems, like the Earth's actual weather (rather than a simple model of it)?

As the mathematical physicist reads the situation 'from below', what will often appear to be happening is mere unpredictability. Out of determinism has arisen apparently random behaviour, but the underlying reality is still held to be purely mechanical. Our limited intellectual powers force us scientifically to think from bottom to top, from underlying simplicity to overall complexity, at least initially. Scientists need a manageable starting-point for their discussions, either in terms of elementary constituents or in terms of a model of abstracted simplicity. We are not clever enough to start with complexity. A mathematician readily grasps the simple rule defining the Mandelbrot set and then comes upon that set's unlimited richness of structure with great surprise. No one, not even Mandelbrot himself, has the ability to start with the set, to grasp it *ab initio*. Analogously, when we talk about the structure of matter, we start with the simplicities of elementary particle physics rather than the complexities of the theory of condensed matter or of biology.

Our thought is constrained to a one-way reading of the story, in which the higher emerges from the lower. In consequence the latter retains its hold upon our mind as controlling the metaphysical picture. It is by no means clear that this is more than a trick of intellectual perspective. In other words, the characteristics of the elementary level (whether deterministic, or quantum mechanical, or whatever) may be as much emergent properties (in the direction of increasing simplicity) as are life or consciousness (in the direction of increasing complexity). Subatomic particles are not only not 'more real' than a bacterial cell; they also have no greater privileged share in determining the nature of reality. That structured chaos can arise from deterministic equations is a mathematical fact. That fact by itself does not settle the metaphysical question of whether the future is determined or, on the contrary, the world is open in its process.

It might, perhaps, be suggested that quantum theory has already settled that issue for us. The most widely held interpretation of that theory's meaning regards individual quantum events as being radically random, so that when the wavefunction 'collapses' on to one of the possible results of a macroscopic observation, the process of the physical world has taken a turn in a particular and intrinsically novel direction.[15] Something unforeseeable has come about. The apparent regularity of so much macroscopic experience is held simply to be the statistical effect of the law of large numbers, the essentially predictable average of many stochastic events. One might then go on to suppose that, in the case of macroscopic systems in regimes of chaotic behaviour, their exquisite sensitivity to detailed circumstance would effectively enmesh them in a microscopic world of quantum uncertainty. (In attempting prediction one would soon reach levels of required accuracy which are denied to us by Heisenberg's uncertainty principle.) Thus the openness of physical process would seem to have been established, even from a bottom-up point of view. In fact, the matter is more complicated than that, for three reasons.

The first complication relates to the character of quantum physics. If one takes a foundational view of the role of elementary particles, then the Schrödinger equation is the true equation, rather than any of those proposed by classical physics. At the time of writing there is a hot debate about whether this equation generates chaotic behaviour. It is certainly known that the analogues of some systems which are classically chaotic (for example, the so-called 'kicked rotator') are not chaotic quantum mechanically. Intuitively one might conjecture that this had something to do with quantum fuzziness on length scales of the Compton wavelength and less, which would not permit the infinitely repeating fractal behaviour which seems to be associated with true chaos.[16] It is not known how typical are these quantum systems which have been studied and found not to be chaotic. Perhaps quantum mechanics requires a different characterization of chaotic behaviour from that found to work in classical mechanics. It would be extremely perplexing if chaos were totally absent from the quantum world, especially in the limit as Planck's constant becomes small, where correspondence principle arguments encourage the expectation of recovering classically describable behaviour. Joseph Ford has commented that 'Should chaos not be found in quantum mechanics, then an earthquake in the foundations of physics appears inevitable, say about magnitude twenty on the Richter scale'.[17]

A second reason for caution is that the whole question of the nature of quantum reality is itself still a highly contentious issue. Our discussion so far has been in terms of the mainstream understanding held by most physicists (which I personally share).

There are, however, radically different proposals which also have their supporters. David Bohm's deterministic version is as empirically adequate as the conventional account, even if it appears to many to be unpersuasively contrived. The many-worlds interpretation holds that everything that can happen, does happen, even if that implies many alternative yet realized histories for the universe. I am not at all convinced by either of these options, but they remain on the metaphysical table and so they put question marks against any simple claim that quantum theory by itself establishes the openness of physical process.

A third complication relates to an unresolved problem in the interpretation of quantum theory. How does a fitful theory yield a definite observational answer each time it is investigated experimentally? The measurement problem in quantum theory has received no agreed solution but among the possibilities being canvassed is one which would see quantum theory itself as a downward-emergent approximation to a more complex physical reality. The matter is somewhat technical, and certainly contentious, so I have relegated its discussion to a note at the end of this chapter (see also Chapter 7).

These considerations lead one to be cautious about invoking quantum theory to establish the openness of macroscopic process. We are encouraged to go on to inquire about the possibility of augmenting bottom-up thinking by intellectual traffic in the opposite direction. Accordingly, I return to the question of whether some of the characteristics discerned in low level exploration of the world (basic physics) may not be regarded as emergent at that level, so that they need not be made universally prescriptive for metaphysics. To address the issue bluntly: if apparently open behaviour is associated with underlying apparently deterministic equations, which is to be taken to have the greater ontological seriousness – the behaviour or the equations? Which is the approximation and which is the reality? It is conceivable that apparent determinism emerges at some lower levels without its being a characteristic of reality overall. For instance it might arise from the approximation of treating subsystems as if they were isolatable from the whole, which in fact they are not, as subsequent discussion will show (p. 43). But first let us consider a philosophical argument.

I take a critically realist view of our scientific exploration of the world. Such a position implies the possibility of gaining verisimilitudinous knowledge, which is reliable without claiming to be exhaustive. In that case, what we know and what is the case are believed to be closely allied; epistemology and ontology are intimately connected. One can see how natural this view is for a scientist by considering the early history of quantum theory. Heisenberg's famous discussion of thought experiments, such as the gamma-ray microscope, dealt with what can be measured. It was an epistemological analysis. Yet for the majority of physicists it led to ontological conclusions. They interpret the uncertainty principle as not being merely a principle of ignorance (as Bohm, for example, would interpret it) but as a principle of genuine indeterminacy. In an analogous way, it seems to me to be a coherent possibility to interpret the undoubted unpredictability of so much of physical process as indicating that process to be ontologically open.

The option is there, but it is not, of course, a forced move to choose it. The case for doing so is greatly enhanced if one acknowledges the necessity of describing a physical world of which we can see ourselves as inhabitants. There are, of course, metaphysical traditions which deny that necessity. Cartesian dualism draws a sharp distinction between a realm of pure extension, in which even animals are only automata, and the human realm of minds-in-bodies. I have elsewhere given reasons for rejecting that picture and attempting to replace it with a complementary mind/matter metaphysic which sees the world-stuff as being in an emergent-downwards mode the matter of which physics speaks, and in an emergent-upward mode the mind that we experience (the direction being that of increasing complexity and flexibility of organization).[18] There is some relation here with the thought of Jürgen Moltmann, innocent as it is of any detailed concern for scientific insight. In his discussion of what it can mean in the Creed to say that God is the Creator of 'heaven and earth', Moltmann decides that creation is an open system and 'We call the determined side of this system "earth", the undetermined side "heaven" '.[19] One might say that 'earth' is process read downwards towards determinism, 'heaven' is process read upwards towards participation in spiritual reality.

There are also metaphysical traditions which deny that the incorporation of humanity into their scheme requires any relaxation of a deterministic picture. Hence the age-old philosophical debate concerning free will and determinism. This is not the place in which to attempt a detailed discussion of these issues. Donald MacKay was prepared to argue that, even if one conceded that the world was deterministic (a concession which he did not necessarily endorse but which might have been more congenial to his Calvinist theology, with its rigid notion of God's sovereignty, than would be the case with my own theological thinking), nevertheless there would still be a logical independence of the personal I-story in relation to the scientific O-story,[20] which would allow a kind of squaring-of-the-circle in permitting both a determinist account (O) and an open account (I) of reality. I do not believe that this approach succeeds. I do believe that, in the end, the denial of human freedom is incoherent, because it destroys rationality. On its own terms, its very utterance, though purporting to be reasoned, is no more than the mouthing of an automaton. Like all extreme critiques born of the hermeneutics of suspicion, it ultimately proves to be suicidal.

A consequence of the delicate sensitivity of complex dynamical systems to circumstance is that they are not only unpredictable but also intrinsically unisolatable. A favourite example to illustrate this is provided by considering collisions of gas molecules, treated as if they were tiny classical billiard balls. (Of course, they are not, but the model is a good one for many purposes.) So rapidly do the effects of initial uncertainties exponentiate in the course of a sequence of collisions, that at normal temperature and pressure the 50 or so collisions that take place for each molecule in the space of only 10^{-10} seconds, would differ significantly in their outcome if there were an unconsidered electron (the smallest particle of matter) on the other side of the observable universe (the furthest distance away) interacting through its gravitational attraction (the weakest of the fundamental forces of nature). Even so simple a system as air, in a period as short as less than a milli-micro-second, would require universal knowledge for its adequate fine-grained discussion. Once again we are given cause for caution in accepting that a bottom-up, intrinsically atomistic description of nature is a sufficient basis for metaphysics. The notion of a set of isolated basic entities is a highly abstracted idea. As an elementary particle physicist, I do not question the utility of the notion for some purposes, only its adequacy for all.

That message is reinforced by further consideration of the quantum world itself. I now look to aspects of the subject which are not matters of disputed interpretation, like some of those considered earlier. Whatever one's views on those issues, the theoretical analyses of John Bell and the experimental investigations of Alain Aspect and his collaborators have made it clear that there is an inescapable non-locality involved in the phenomena.[21] Quantum entities exhibit a counterintuitive togetherness-in-separation, a power once they have interacted to influence each other however far they subsequently separate. Paradoxically, the atomic world is one that cannot be described atomistically. A very careful and lucid discussion of the issues that this raises has been given by Bernard d'Espagnat.[22] He is emphatic that philosophy must take account of what physics has to tell it. 'We may imagine that to reach the truth we only need to come up with brilliant ideas' but that is mistaken for 'it remains illusory to hope that in our day people can still make valid claims on matters such as reality, time and causality, if these claims are not rooted in the extraordinarily elaborate factual knowledge now at our disposal'.[23] d'Espagnat is a realist, for he feels that denial of an independent reality leads to the danger of collapse into solipsism, a person being driven to retreat into the sole refuge of his own thinking mind. Yet quantum theory denies the possibility of embracing a naive and particulate objectivity in our account of the physical world. d'Espagnat summarizes the dilemma:

> It was once thought [for example by positivism] that the notion of being must be repudiated. Now that it has finally become apparent that to do so is to court incoherence, it is dismaying to find that in the interim it has become peculiarly difficult, if facts are to be respected, to rehabilitate that notion.[24]

His solution is to speak of independent reality as 'veiled' and to be distinguished from empirical reality. That sounds at first like a proposal to move in a Kantian direction of discriminating between phenomena (things as they appear) and noumena (things in themselves), but d'Espagnat does not go all the way with Kant. He insists that independent reality is veiled rather than inaccessible; it is elusive rather than absolutely unknowable. He wishes (as I do too) to give all due weight to the insights of physics but he also acknowledges that 'It does not seem incoherent to me to admit the possibility of rational activity that does not issue in "demonstrative certainty" in the sense we scientists use the expression'.[25] Because I feel very strongly that this is so (see Chapter 1), I am driven to greater metaphysical boldness than d'Espagnat will permit himself. Nevertheless, I believe that his cautious invocation of veiledness is, at the least, not inconsistent with the kind of openness about the nature of reality which I am trying to explore.

The picture which has been building up is that of a physical world liberated from the thrall of the merely mechanical but retaining those orderly elements which science has been so successful in exhibiting and understanding. In Popper's famous metaphor, it is a world of clouds and clocks, in which some things are indeed predictable but others are open to the possibility of new development. I have elsewhere argued that such a world of intertwined order and novelty is just that which might be expected as the creation of a God both faithful and loving, who will endow his world with the twin gifts of reliability and freedom.[26]

In a bottom-up description of the physical world, the onset of flexible openness is signalled by the myriad possibilities of future development which present themselves to a complex dynamical system. In a quasi-determinist account they arise from the greatly differing trajectories which would result from initial conditions differing only infinitesimally from each other. Because of their undifferentiable proximity of circumstance, there is no energetic discrimination between these possibilities. The 'choice' of path actually followed corresponds, not to the result of some physically causal act (in the sense of an energy input) but rather to a 'selection' from options (in the sense of an information input). One might well be able to formalize the last point. Typically the open options can be expressed in terms of bifurcating possibilities (this or that), whose particular realizations resemble bits of information (switches on or off, in a crude computer analogy). In a top-down description of systems of such complexity as ourselves, this 'information input' is a picture of how mind could operate causally within a complementary mind/matter metaphysic. Because flexibility only arises within intrinsically unpredictable circumstances, the springs of the operation of mind would be inescapably hidden ('veiled'). The search for a modern equivalent of the Cartesian pineal gland would be the search for a will-o'-the-wisp; it is condemned to failure.

It is by no means clear that information input of the kind described originates solely from animals, humankind, and whatever similar agents there might be. I do not believe that God is contained within the mind/matter confines of the world,[27] but it is entirely conceivable that he might interact with it (both in relation to humanity and in relation to all other open process) in the form of information input. I have attempted elsewhere to explore some of the theological consequences of such a view, particularly in relation to questions of prayer and theodicy.[28] God is not pictured as an interfering agent among other agencies. (That would correspond to energy input.) Instead, form is given to the possibility that he influences his creation in a non-energetic way. Many theological writers have recoiled from the detachment of deism and have wished to assert an interactive relationship between God and the world. They have been notably coy, however, about how this might actually come about. Austin Farrer's account of double agency is so emphatic about the inscrutability of the divine side of it as to provide us with no help.[29] The various varieties of panentheism (asserting the world to be part of God, but not the whole of him) afford no more than an image of divine action - and an unsatisfactory one at that, in my opinion.[30] Arthur Peacocke has offered us the picture of God as 'an Improviser of unsurpassed ingenuity',[31] seeking to incorporate the discords of evil into a greater harmony, but how that Great Improviser actually touches the keyboard is not made clear. The idea of divine interaction through information input seems to me to afford us some help in the matter.[32]

The view I am proposing has been criticized by some reviewers of its earlier articulation, as being a return to the discredited notion of a God of the gaps. I disagree. One must be careful not to be carried away by verbal analogies, more apparent than real. If there is any free action (human or divine), it seems to me that there will have to be 'gaps' or openesses in physical process, as it is described from the bottom up. The correct lower-level description can only provide an envelope of possibility within which top-down causation will find its scope for realization. We are 'people of the gaps' in this sense and it is surely not an error for God's interaction to be thought of in an analogous way, for the gaps to which we are now referring are intrinsic. They contrast with the arbitrary gaps of the old-style argument, which were simply patches of current ignorance, with no enduring status attached to them. Of course, the ideas I am presenting here are speculative, but we have to be bold enough to make some venture in the matter. Otherwise, talk of top-down causation (however phrased) is no more than the utterance of slogans whose conceivable validity is completely unclear.

The picture here being suggested of the mode of God's interaction with his creation, over and above his great act of sustaining it in being, might seem to bear some cousinly relation to the notions of process theology, which built upon the metaphysical scheme elaborated by A. N. Whitehead.[33] The latter takes as its fundamental entities 'events', and each event has a dual character, possessing a kind of psychic pole (prehension) in which a 'choice' of possibilities is made, followed by a material pole (concrescence) in which the selected option is realized. In process theology, God's action is in the form of a lure, a continuing attempt to entice the world in a certain direction, although in Whitehead's view all true initiative lies with the world itself in acts of concrescence. He reacted violently against the classical picture of God as a 'cosmic tyrant', tightly in control of all that happens, but to many he has seemed to end up with what Eric Mascall wittily called the picture of a God more to be pitied than to be worshipped, as he stands pleading from the sidelines of the world.

I do not think that Whitehead's episodic scheme of a concatenation of events (so that entities are secondary constructs made out of strings of events) is at all persuasive. Though it might bear some superficial resemblance to the occasional fitfulness found in quantum measurement, it fails to accommodate a concept like that of a quantum field, whose essence is the combination of quantum discreteness with the continuity characteristic of a field. Nor do I find the implicit panpsychism involved in talk of prehension to be at all congenial or convincing.

The metaphysical scheme espoused in this chapter succeeds, in my opinion, in retaining some of the more attractive features of process thought without its defects. It is a kind of demythologization of that panpsychic world-view. God is certainly not a cosmic tyrant; his interaction with his world can be expected to respect its freedom (including our own).[34] His acts will be veiled within the unpredictability of complex process. They may be discernible by faith but they will not be demonstrable by experiment. God is not condemned solely to the role of a passive pleader, which is his fate in process thought, but he is able to act. The flexibility in what happens is not assigned to the operation of a mysterious psychic pole in each material event. Instead it arises naturally from what we have been able to discern scientifically about the nature of physical process. I do not claim that age-old problems are solved. Simply that there is a hopeful way in which we can look at them, whilst retaining the integrity of our experience and understanding in all their aspects: scientific, personal, religious.

A Note on Quantum Measurement
An unresolved problem in the interpretation of quantum theory relates to the act of measurement.[35] The theory itself only predicts the probabilities for a variety of possible outcomes of an act of observation performed on a quantum mechanical system. How does it come about that on any particular occasion when such a measurement is made, that a definite and particular answer is obtained? How does the fitful quantum world interlock with the reliable world of laboratory apparatus to give a specific result?

A variety of proposals, none wholly satisfactory, has been made. The most popular (a form of it was endorsed by Niels Bohr as the received Copenhagen interpretation) assigns the defining role to the intervention of large-scale classical measuring apparatus. The difficulty with this view is that such measuring apparatus is itself made out of quantum constituents. How does this determining property of 'collapsing the wavefunction' (to use the technical phrase) 'emerge' from its indeterminate quantum substrate? The question has not been answered. Posed in this way, it is framed in the spirit of bottom-up thinking, which treats the quantum mechanical as given and the role of the measuring apparatus as the thing to be explained.

A different approach has been suggested by some other physicists (notably Eugene Wigner). Mathematical analysis indicates that the determining role must be played by a system possessing the property of non-linearity, in order to break the linear superposition of a variety of outcomes which is the formal expression of quantum theory's undecidedness. The proposal has not gained wide support, though Roger Penrose has recently argued in favour of such an approach.[36] If it were to prove correct it would be an example of downward emergence. The true equations of physics are held to be non-linear, but in a way that is only significant for large (classical) systems. Conventional quantum theory, and its linearity, would then be an emergent property of small systems.

4 Reason and Revelation

There is a popular caricature which sees the scientist as ever open to the correcting power of new discovery and, in consequence, achieving the reward of real knowledge, whilst the religious believer condemns himself to intellectual imprisonment within the limits of an opinion held on a priori grounds, to which he will cling whatever facts there might be to the contrary. The one is the man of reason; the other blocks the road of honest inquiry with a barrier labelled 'incontestable revelation'. Even a theologian like the New Testament scholar Gerd Theissen seems to accord some credibility to this view: 'scientific thought is subject to falsification, while faith goes against the facts'.[1] If that were really so, those of us who are both scientists and religious believers – and we form a not inconsiderable company – would be living schizophrenically, believing the impossible on Sundays and only opening our minds again on Monday mornings. I do not think that this is the case. The picture is distorted in two ways.

Firstly, it takes too idealized and oversimplified a view of science. It is by no means my aim to win a degree of tolerance for theology by seeking to denigrate science. I am a self-confessed critical realist who believes that, through the verisimilitude achieved by well-winnowed physical theories,[2] we have learnt many things of the greatest significance about the world in which we live. Yet we have also to recognize the subtlety of the scientific method. It does not provide us with a unique 'methodological threshing machine in which the flail of experiment separates the grain of truth from the chaff of error'.[3] Acts of judgement are involved which give science a cousinly relationship with other forms of human inquiry, including theology (see Chapter 1).[4] An act of faith is necessary for the scientist: a commitment to the metaphysical belief that the world is intelligible and open to our rational exploration. Such a belief can be motivated by the testimony of generations that it has been found to be so, but it has also been severely threatened at times when the 'facts' have seemed to go against it. The most striking examples of this derive from the history of quantum physics. The character of light, sometimes particle-like, sometimes wave-like, gave rise to great perplexity until quantum field theory achieved a rationally harmonious understanding, free from contradiction. The still-unresolved questions of the interpretation of quantum mechanics (in particular the notion, espoused in some understandings of what is going on, that individual quantum events are 'uncaused') continue to make some uneasy. For sixty years fundamental physics has lived with two of its foundational theories – quantum mechanics and general relativity – imperfectly reconciled with each other. At the more humdrum level of detailed agreement with experiment, it is a commonplace that seldom has a scientific theory fitted perfectly all the claimed results with which it had to deal, although quantum electrodynamics – described by the late Richard Feynman as 'the jewel in the crown of physics' – comes nearest in its circumscribed domain to that achievement.[5] It would certainly not have been a fruitful strategy in science to throw in the towel at the first encounter with problematic data. A certain degree of courageous persistence, open to the possibility of correction but not prone to the hasty dismantling of theories well-winnowed by experience, has been the way in which further understanding has most frequently been achieved. John Wheeler has rightly characterized the style of science as 'radical conservatism', an approach which is both reluctant to introduce new assumptions and also determined to press its current ideas as hard and as far as they will go.[6]

Secondly, the caricature presents a picture of religious thought that is also misleading. It seems to equate the latter with fideism – the bare assertion that something is so as a matter of faith, needing no element of rational inquiry for its support. Of course, it is impossible to deny that some religious people have adopted such a stance. In the ancient world, one thinks of Tertullian, stoutly but perversely maintaining that he believed 'because it is impossible'. In the modern world, Martin Gardner, though standing outside all historic traditions, proclaims himself to be a fideist, saying that 'wherever I speak of religious faith it will mean a belief, unsupported by logic or science'. Later he goes on to speak of faith as 'nonrational belief'.[7] In due course I shall wish to submit these claims to critical examination. In the meantime let us also acknowledge the existence of quite widespread forms of covert fideism, which have the similitude of open inquiry without the substance. There are certain kinds of biblical study, let us say in relation to questions of historical reliability or authorship, in which one feels that there is a hidden agenda, proscribing from the outset certain kinds of answer. By no means all these covert instances involve only those of a conservative cast of mind. There is a 'horizontal fideism' of liberal origin which casts itself quite as uncritically upon the spirit of the age as does the 'vertical fideism'

50

of fundamentalism upon its assumption of divinely guaranteed information. Equally the sad excesses of 'creation science' so-called (which seem to me to illustrate in the clearest possible way how a slanted and selective perspective can be imposed by a priori requirements) have a matching counterpart in the wilful reductionism of those who espouse, not science, but scientism, and so close their eyes to the rich complexity which makes up actual experience. Someone like Peter Atkins is a fideist.[8]

It is time to take a second look at Martin Gardner. He speaks of religious belief as being 'unsupported by logic or science'. To accept that at face value would be to deny any possibility of a natural theology, an inquiry which one might define as the attempt to learn something of God through the exercise of reason and the general exploration of the world. That is a concession that I, for one, would not be prepared to make. On the contrary, I believe that we are living at a time of a revival of natural theology, a movement, interestingly enough, originating more at the hands of the scientists than the theologians.[9] Yet I also acknowledge that the revived natural theology of our day is more modest in its tone than its predecessors of earlier centuries. It speaks of insight rather than demonstration. Its aim is not the classic goal of proving the existence of God. Rather, it seeks to exhibit theism as providing a coherent and deeply intellectually satisfying understanding of the total way things are.[10]

We need not regret this change, for strict proof is a concept of only limited validity. Even mathematics has been found to have its logical Achilles' heel, ever since Gödel showed its consistency to be a question beyond our powers to demonstrate. If by 'support' Gardner meant anything as inexorable as proof, then religious belief would find itself in very extensive company – including, ironically, science itself. Once we leave behind, as we must do, requirements of strict entailment, we enter a realm where, by the exercise of judgement, beliefs can be motivated, but those who refuse to see it that way cannot peremptorily be condemned as perverse or moronic. In these circumstances, we face a choice between two basic approaches: the strategy of suspicion or the strategy of commitment. The former counsels caution and examines the teeth of every intellectual gift horse offered it by human inquiry; the latter takes the risk of intellectual adventure, open to correction but prepared to bet upon the ultimate fruitfulness of rational investigation. In relation to science, the strategy of suspicion engenders the various irrational accounts of scientific activity,[11] whilst the strategy of commitment is the basis for a critical realist philosophy, embraced by almost all practising scientists.[12] If one were to equate the rational with the purely deductive, then (Karl Popper's heroic endeavours notwithstanding) I think one would have to classify science as 'nonrational belief'.[13] Since I regard the latter judgement as unacceptable, I believe that there is a broad territory of rationally motivated belief, lying between absolute certainty on the one hand and irrational assertion on the other, in which both science and theology are located (see Chapter 1). If one were to take the strictest sense of 'know' (that is, to know beyond a peradventure) then both science and theology call for that act of faith which Gardner defined when he spoke of faith as being 'when you believe something you don't know is true'.[14] But that by no means implies that we do not have reasons for accepting the accounts that science and theology offer. Those who only bet on certainties are living unacceptably circumscribed lives.

It is clear, however, that there are greatly differing degrees of difficulty involved in making the intellectual commitment called for in pursuit of the various disciplines about which we have been thinking. Most of us can swallow mathematics without a gulp or tremor. The possibility of its inconsistency keeps few awake at night. Somewhat more contentious is the status of the natural sciences. Hence the philosophical debate to which I have referred. Yet there is an impressive degree of unanimity achieved time and again within the competent community about the answer to some scientific question, once the winnowing process has had the chance to do its sifting work. Who doubts that the blood circulates, that matter is composed of atoms, that DNA is a helical structure made out of four bases? Moreover, these agreements cross many cultural boundaries. Stop any competent person in the street in London, Delhi or Tokyo, and ask them what matter is composed of, and in all three cities you will receive the reply that there is certainly a level of structure corresponding to quarks and gluons and electrons.

How different the situation would be if that scientific question were to be replaced by the religious question: What is the nature of ultimate reality? In all probability one would receive distinctly differing answers from persons accosted in those three cities. Does not that fact alone mean that it is no more than a debating point of dubious value for me to have placed both science and theology in the same broad intellectual territory lying between the certain and the irrational? Is not that territory divided into a zone of publicly accessible fact (containing science) and a zone of privately held opinion (containing religion)?

I would want to characterize the situation differently, in terms

52

of the degree of personal engagement demanded. The more highly personal an encounter, the more critical is its uniqueness and the more its evaluation will call for a judgement that can only be exercised by those actually involved in it. The convincing character of the experimental method in science (to whose power I, as a theoretical physicist, gladly testify) arises from the ability to reproduce, in all relevant essentials, a previously tested situation so that the results then obtained can be subjected to confirmation or contest by other interested parties. It may be true that we never step into the same river twice, but in most situations of interest to science there are many variations of circumstance which can be bracketed out and held to be irrelevant (such as the colour of the experimenter's hair or the state of his digestion). Reaching that conclusion about what is ignorable requires an act of judgement about what is relevant. In addition there are other acts of judgement involved in a scientific interpretation of what is going on. Raw readings are of no interest by themselves and in modern science highly sophisticated interpretative schemes, themselves deeply embedded in the current understanding of the physical world, are necessary to turn data into scientifically significant results. The role of experience and judgement in evaluating experiments, and the creative insights needed for theoretical construction, are reasons why I broadly accept the account of science given by Michael Polanyi, who spoke of its involving 'personal knowledge'.[15] By that he meant that tacit skills are called for which imply that the task could never be delegated to a computer, however cleverly programmed. We are not able to devise the instructions for a Nobel Prize winning automaton because there is an inexhaustible and inaccessible component in scientific judgement, which can only be acquired through apprenticeship. 'We know more than we can tell.'

Science, therefore, is not completely impersonal, but nevertheless it proves capable of achieving a high degree of interpersonal agreement. Important as is the role of great men in its history, there are no grounds for supposing them to be individually indispensable for its progress. Newton's achievements in writing the *Principia* and the *Opticks* are prodigious, but lesser men would have made piecemeal advances leading to the same conclusions if that premature baby, born on Christmas Day 1642, had not survived. In the arts it is different. The death of Beethoven in infancy would have deprived the world of the *Missa Solemnis*.

Generations of physics students have faced essentially the same situations as they worked their way through practical syllabuses. Yet every moral decision has its individual quality, which is one

of the reasons why I believe that serious novels will always continue to be written. There are indeed ethical guidelines, but the
subtleties of weighing moral circumstance preclude the existence
of a compendious rule book in which one may look up the
answer.

Because art and ethics are more deeply personal than science,
they do not represent areas in which universal agreement is
attainable. Individual experiences, and the understandings of them,
differ too greatly for that to be possible. Yet the moral and the
aesthetic seem to me to be realms of human experience to be
taken with the utmost seriousness.[16] I do not want to argue the
case here, but I simply state that a view of the world which regarded
these fundamental insights as being no more than epi-
phenomenal - a kind of froth on the surface of a basically material
and scientifically circumscribable reality - would be profoundly
unconvincing. In saying that, I acknowledge the inescapable degree
to which culturally determined factors enter into judgements in
these matters. Their influence sometimes distorts our vision, but
I believe that it is still a true reality of which we glimpse 'puzzling
reflections in a mirror' (1 Corinthians 13.12, NEB).

More deeply personal still is that realm of human record which
speaks of encounter with the divine, whether in terms of the
mystic's ineffable experience of union with the All, or the numinous encounter with the One standing over against, *tremendum
et fascinans*, or the less dramatic experience of countless religious
people in private prayer and worship. Here the refracting power
of culture will be powerfully present - Christians see visions of
Jesus or the Virgin Mary, Buddhists of the Buddha - and this may
to some extent help us to understand the puzzling diversity of
the world's religions.[17] Even if that is so, many perplexities remain, which are beyond my ability to resolve. Yet, once again, I
claim that it is a true reality of which we glimpse 'puzzling
reflections in a mirror', this time applying St Paul's phrase to its
proper Subject.

We now enter an area of discussion where talk of revelation
appears as a possible entry on the agenda. It is important to make
it clear from the outset that by revelation I do not mean a divinely guaranteed set of propositions made available to us by their
being written on tablets of stone, or whispered into the mental
ear of the human writers of Scripture, or infallibly endorsed by a
General Council of Bishops. Much as I respect Scripture and
the tradition of the Church, it seems to me that their characters
are misunderstood if they are conceived of in such an incorrigible and literalist fashion. Take, for example, the catholic creeds

(Apostles' and Nicene) recognized by almost all Christians as *symbola*, expressions of the faith. Firstly, they are strikingly compact, as condensed in form as the mathematical formulae expressing a physical law. They use a specialized vocabulary which requires as much unpacking as would the equations of physics. I believe that what has been boiled down in these concise credal statements is not unbridled metaphysical speculation but the distillation of Christian experience.[18] They do not 'go against the facts'; rather, they are mnemonic summaries of the facts – the experience of the Fatherhood of God through prayer, the impossibility of speaking adequately of Jesus and the aftermath of his death other than in terms of life and divinity, the mysterious but undeniable working within ourselves of a Power beyond ourselves. Yet compared with a scientific formulation like, say, Maxwell's equations, the creeds are limited in the success of their descriptive task. Maxwell's equations encapsulate perfectly the structure of electromagnetism and they have remained unaltered in form for more than a hundred years, despite changing usage corresponding to scientific developments, such as the transition from classical to quantum mechanics. God is not so to be delineated by any formula. To suppose the contrary is to fall into the sin of idolatry.

So how can the Infinite reveal himself to finite creatures without obliterating the recipients of his glorious manifestation by the sheer weight of his presence? Christianity propounds an astonishing – I would want to say, a breathtakingly exciting – answer: By focusing the Infinite upon the finite in the life of a human being, by making himself known in the plainest possible terms by living the life of a man in Jesus Christ. This is not the occasion to undertake, even in the most summary form,[19] a discussion of why I think this astounding claim is believable. Let me simply comment on the consequence of its acceptance. It destroys any flat, matter-of-fact, notion of revelation, for the true divine self-expression, the Word of God, is not a proposition but a person. Its eternal utterance is not the foreclosing of rational inquiry but an invitation to personal encounter. Martin Buber has emphasized the difference between I-It relationships and I-Thou relationships.[20] The former confine us to an objective externalized world surveyed by a detached observer (who is the rational ego of Cartesian thought). Such a world might indeed be reified and its understanding reduced to propositional form. The latter demands the openness of full personal knowledge. It can never be summarized by detached statements but it can be known only by taking the risk, and embracing the ambiguity, of encounter. 'Egos appear by setting themselves apart from other egos. Persons appear by entering into relation with other persons.'[21] For the Christian, the figure of Christ is the focal point for the meeting of the divine and the human, the One in relation to whom we will come to know God most fully.

Yet if we feel we recognize in Jesus elements which for their proper appreciation call for the use of the language of divinity, then we already have some concept of God by which to make that identification (even if it is then expanded and corrected by the encounter with Christ). There is a theological tradition, associated in this century particularly with the name of Karl Barth, which denies that possibility. It states that God is known solely through his self-revelation in Christ; rational inquiry elsewhere has no role whatsoever to play in true encounter with the divine. That is not a position that I find myself able to accept.[22] But where then is God to be sought? The obvious answer would seem to be in the varieties of religious experience, but a recent book by Nicholas Lash, concerned with presenting 'reflections on human experience and the knowledge of God', sounds a note of caution. Lash proposes 'to argue, on the one hand, that it is not the case that all experience of God is necessarily religious in form or content and, on the other hand, that not everything which it would be appropriate to characterize, on psychological or sociological grounds, as "religious" experience would thereby necessarily constitute experience of God'.[23] The root of the difficulty, it seems to me, lies in the nature of God. He is not an entity among other entities, concerning whom one can say 'Lo, here' or 'Lo, there', thus locating him within some circumscribed religious domain. Rather, he is the source of all that is, the One omnipresent to every human experience. There is no possibility of identifying his presence by contrasting it with the different experience of his absence. Yet to rest on that theological fact alone would risk attenuating our understanding of the divine to a merely deistic notion of the sustaining ground of all. The steadfast consistency of God in relation to his creation is not to be confused with a dreary uniformity. He is not just Someone who does nothing in particular, even if it were conceded that he did it very well. A personal God, such as that of which Christianity speaks, must be capable of specific response to specific circumstance, for otherwise, as David Brown says, 'it would seem misleading to characterize what is going on as a personal relationship at all'.[24]

If everything is sacramental, the idea of sacrament is in danger of becoming vacuous. Lash quotes a comment of Patrick Sherry's concerning Baron von Hügel's emphasis on the pervasiveness of the sense of the presence of God, that 'the experience, as described by him, is so general that it is not clear what it would be like *not* to have such an experience'.[25] We have to consider, therefore, what sense can be made of the notion of particular revelatory events.

Perhaps we can gain some small degree of insight by comparing the knowledge of God with our knowledge of the laws of nature. The comparison is not quite as far-fetched as it may seem. I believe that the regularities of natural law are pale reflections of the consistency of the One who is their Ordainer. Willy-nilly, we all have experience of the force of gravity, but to know that we do requires a particular way of looking at the world. Only when the apple fell in the orchard at Woolsthorpe (if legend be true), did it occur to someone to ask whether the force that brought about that falling was the same force that held the Moon in its orbit round the Earth. Lash quotes a remark of Karl Rahner's that 'the answer given in revelation *clarifies* the question a man asks'.[26] The recognition of the divine implies viewing the world in a certain perspective, the adoption of a theistic point of view which brings enlightenment where previously there was opacity to understanding. We need to know the questions that are profitable to address. A good deal of the skill of the successful scientist lies in asking the right questions. In both science and theology there is a dialogue between interpretation and experience, which react dialectically upon each other. Lash says that 'experience is *modified* by the interpretations that we offer, the memories to which we appeal in the stories that we tell'.[27] I would prefer to say that a possible significance is made accessible to us by these means. In neither science nor theology are we just imposing a point of view upon supposedly plastic experience, moulding it into shapes pleasing to our individual or communal tastes. (I take Lash's cautious word 'modified' to imply rejection of the notion, asserted by adherents of the strong programme in the sociology of knowledge,[28] that world views are simply social agreements to see it that way.) In both science and theology we are seeking a scheme of understanding in which interpretation and experience match with the most satisfying consonance and economy. The enforcement of this maximal coherence provides reasonable grounds for making a choice between differing possibilities. I believe this method to be the essence of rational inquiry into the way things are (see Chapter 1).

Gravity is always there, but to perceive and understand it we need not only to adopt the appropriate point of view and ask the appropriate questions; we need also to have access to specially simple situations in which we can study its nature. People have speculated whether the equivalent Newtonian revelation could have taken place on a planet which was orbiting a double star. In that case the patterns of gravitationally controlled motion would have been so complex that their unravelling might well have defied the efforts of a succession of Sir Isaacs.[29] Gravity is always there, but its character is only made transparent in very particular circumstances.

Perhaps this observation offers us some understanding of why there are particular moments in history, or particular people, or particular incidents in the lives of individuals, which have a character in terms of their openness to the experience and knowledge of God that causes them to be spoken of as occasions of revelation.

The great religious traditions will look particularly to their foundational revelatory experiences, just as a scientific discipline like nuclear physics looks back to Rutherford's pioneering investigations in 1911 which first revealed the existence of a concentration of positive charge at the heart of an atom, which we now call the nucleus. Yet there are many moments of divine disclosure (recognized as such or not; described in religious terms or not) in the lives of many people.[30] The Religious Experience Unit founded by Sir Alister Hardy has done some interesting surveys which reveal how these occasions are much more widespread, even in this secular age, than might have been supposed.[31] Michael Pafford collected 'Excerpts from Autobiographies with Hints and Guesses', drawing on writers as diverse as St Augustine and Bertrand Russell. He called the experiences so recorded 'unattended moments', flashes of insight which seemed to point to a dimension of reality beyond that of the everyday, 'echoes of that twilight *terra incognita* beyond the limits where words fail though meanings may exist'.[32]

By no means all would want to use theistic language in speaking about these experiences. How then can I take it upon myself to foist it on them? I think that God is necessarily veiled in his encounter with finite humanity and so it would not be altogether surprising if the veil proved impenetrable for many, but the character of what they say is so similar to that which religious believers speak of as being divine that I cannot doubt that it is the same Reality that is encountered. But how do I know that Reality is God – that the capital R is justified? Nicholas Lash poses the question 'if some people find themselves to stand in relation to whatever they consider to be God, how do they know that it is *God* with whom they are in relation? It must surely be on the basis of an idea of God obtained from somewhere else that they decide that *this* experience, this feeling, is experience of God'. He goes on to quote Kant, who said that 'The Concept of God and the conviction of His existence can be met with only in reason; they can come from reason alone, not from either inspiration or any tidings, however great their authority'.[33]

I doubt whether that is right. If there is a God, who possesses aseity (being-in-itself), then he is self-authenticating; he does not call for evaluation by any other criteria. That seems to be the message at the end of the Book of Job. Despite that poor and suffering man's desire to argue his case with God, when the Lord speaks to him out of the whirlwind, that utterance is itself sufficient answer. 'I had heard of thee by the hearing of the ear, but now my eye sees thee; therefore I despise myself and repent in dust and ashes' (Job 42.5-6).

One sees how dangerous this is. A homicidal maniac hears the voice of God telling him to go out and kill prostitutes. That is why religion is not what one does with one's solitariness, why it can only be pursued within a community and following a tradition, with the correctives they apply to private judgement. We need always to take account of what has been experienced and understood by other people and other ages, before we conclude that here we stand and can do no other. 'Test everything; hold fast to what is good' (1 Thessalonians 5.21). Yet, ultimately, the One who is the Ground of all reality, is to be known in himself, the Subject of worship and not the object of scrutiny.

It is time to draw this tentative sketch of the comparison between scientific reason and Christian revelation to a close. I deny an opposition between an open-minded science and a closed, incorrigible religion. Both, in fact, are concerned with seeking to describe the nature of reality. The difference between them is not that between reasonableness and obscurantism. It lies, rather, in the nature of the aspects of reality that they are seeking to explore. One is concerned with the physical world, which we transcend and can manipulate. The other is concerned with One who transcends us in his love and mercy. Both incorporate appeal to experience. Science looks for the grounds of its understanding to experiments which are within its power to contrive. Religion depends upon those revelatory moments of divine disclosure which cannot be brought about by human will alone but which come as a gracious gift.

5 The Use of Scripture

Those of us who write about the traffic across the border between science and religion are sometimes reprimanded by reviewers, usually of an evangelical persuasion, for paying insufficient attention to the Bible. It is not being suggested that the answers to modern scientific questions are to be found within its covers – for the curious and disturbing phenomenon of 'scientific creationism' is scarcely to be encountered in Britain, however much it may rampage on the other side of the Atlantic – but rather that questions of reason and reality should be judged from a standpoint controlled by Scripture. Here, it is proposed, lies the key to theological interpretative problems. Stated bluntly like that, the proposal seems to short-circuit an obvious difficulty. I gladly acknowledge the importance of Scripture for Christian life and thought, but how is it actually to be used? The briefest acquaintance with the history of the Church makes it plain that a variety of methods have been employed, from the narrowest literalism to the most fantastic allegorization, from reliance upon isolated proof texts to the most generalized notion of a record of evolving religious consciousness. As part of our exercise of reason in the pursuit of reality we have to consider what is the proper usage of the Christian Scriptures.

At the outset, let me say that one of the reasons why detailed attention to the Bible may play only a subsidiary role in much writing about science and theology is that such writing itself plays only an auxiliary role in relation to the great endeavour of the intellectual exploration of Christian faith. I do not say that such writing is not of importance – for me it is an essential task to hold together my scientific and Christian insights with as much integrity as I can muster, and to some extent that must be true for those who are not themselves scientists but who live in a culture in which science is a significant component. I do say, however, that considerations of natural theology and the like do not afford the fundamental basis for my own religious belief. That lies in my encounter with God in Christ, mediated through the Church, the sacraments, and, of course, the reading of Scripture. The discussion of science-and-religion is a valuable but second-order task, in which one seeks an harmonious integration of one's basic experiences as a believer and as a scientist. In a sense it is a fringe activity, selecting from each area those elements which lie closest to the other, and not necessarily reflecting more than a part of that subject's central preoccupations. One no more expects to get from such writing a balanced account of theology than one supposes its discussion of science to represent an even-handed survey of the physical world. In each case, the material selected is chosen with the other discipline in mind.

I have already acknowledged that the Bible is important to me in my own religious life. There is a strong tradition of Christian thought which assigns it a supreme role, making the Bible the arbiter of all theological inquiry. A conservative biblicism has often proved attractive to scientists, particularly in their student days. They are familiar with the notion of the textbook, that reliable source of information in which one can look up the answer to one's queries. Much painful labour can be avoided in that way, and there is a certain attraction in the feeling that God should have provided just such a textbook to help us with our religious search. Those who go on to postgraduate scientific study learn that even in the physical world our explorations do not always lead us to cut-and-dried answers. We are not on our own, for we benefit from the accumulated experience and discovery of the scientific community, and its record in the libraries, but even the most assiduous perusal of the pages of the Physical Review will not tell us all that we need to know. The search for truth involves more than the ability to scan the literature.

It is important to recognize that, though almost all Christians down the centuries have assigned a significant and normative role to Scripture, they have not been 'people of the book' in the way that our Islamic friends are, who regard the Koran as a divinely dictated document (and so only properly to be read in the original classical Arabic), or even in the way of Rabbinic Judaism, with its appeal to the Torah (however overlaid with Talmudic interpretation, understood as deriving from a parallel oral tradition). The classic Christian attitude to the Bible has been a subtle mixture of respect and freedom, and it was so from the beginning. Jesus contrasts the creation ordinance of marriage as the union of husband and wife in one flesh with the Mosaic ordinance permitting divorce, and adjudicates in favour of the former (Mark 10.2-9). In the Sermon on the Mount he quotes what 'was said to the men of old' (in fact, in the Torah) and deepens or radicalizes it ('But I say to you...') (Matthew 5). John Barton writes of Paul's use of the Hebrew scriptures in his epistles that

The messianic status of Jesus, his eschatological significance, his death and resurrection and the salvation they have accomplished, these are not argued from scriptural proofs. And yet Paul remains convinced that the Old Scriptures are the Word of God... Very few of the texts he does cite and discuss are chosen because of a 'prophecy and fulfilment' scheme. Often he will bring in an Old Testament text merely to support an argument reached by other routes - this is specially common in his sections of ethical teaching. In them there is not much to choose between the way he cites Scripture and the way he cites popular proverbs or commonplaces.[1]

Even in Matthew's Gospel, the New Testament writing apparently most imbued with a prophecy-and-fulfilment theme, the appeal to Scripture is so curious and selective (even including one verse (Matthew 2.23) which isn't there) that one feels that it is the story of Jesus which is being read into the Old Testament, rather than that story being controlled by what was already there. (I know some scholars take a different view, but it seems hard to believe that oddly assorted selection of texts to be a tail that wagged a dog.) It appears to have been important to the writer to establish a connection with the Old Testament (that is where respect comes in) but the way in which it is done is controlled by something greater, namely the encounter with Christ (and that is where freedom comes in).

In our day, the New Testament is one of the great vehicles which bring about our encounter with Christ. For the Christian the true Word of God is written, not with paper and ink, but in the flesh and blood of that life lived in Palestine long ago (John 1.14) and in the continuing life of the Risen Lord. All authority rests with him (Matthew 28.18) and it is not located between the covers of any book. Yet it is from the Bible that we shall learn much of Jesus and of the life of Israel into which he entered. 'We can account adequately for the position that Scripture holds in the Christian faith only on the basis of a belief that God was genuinely and uniquely known in Israel and was then made more profoundly known in Jesus Christ.'[2] Because revelation is the encounter with a Person and not the deliverance of a set of propositions (see Chapter 4), the Bible is not our divinely-guaranteed textbook but a prime means by which we come to know God's dealings with humankind and particularly his self-utterance in Christ.

A number of things then follow. The first is that there will be an evidential role for Scripture. It is necessary for us to have grounds for the belief that God was in Christ, and it is important for us to know what Jesus was like. 'The Bible matters, to put it at its simplest, because it is the earliest and most compelling evidence that Jesus rose from the dead, and that he was such a person that his rising from the dead is gospel, good news.'[3] As James Barr has said: 'Few would be willing to rest content with a Jesus who in historical fact was an unprincipled crook, a used-chariot salesman of the time'.[4] Many theologians recoil from acknowledging this historico-evidential role for Scripture. They would prefer its being regarded as kerygmatic, the proclamation of a saving faith to be accepted as transcendentally given (Barth) or to be embraced existentially (Bultmann). Otherwise they fear that what should be timeless truth is hazarded upon the uncertain judgement of historians as to what actually happened. But the religion of the incarnation is based on the idea that the Eternal made himself known in the contingency of the temporal, taking the risk of an involvement with human history (Philippians 2.6-8). However moving the story, *simply as story* it is not enough. We need to know it happened. It is instinctive for the scientist to ask the question 'What is the evidence? What makes you think it is actually the case?'

The hermeneutics of suspicion has presented our generation with a temptation to take refuge from history in evoking the power of language, to rest content with the 'language event'. 'The classical mind says that's only a story, but the modern mind says, there's only story.'[5] I am not willing to resign so easily from the cognitive quest. I cannot accept the view, described by Northrop Frye, that 'The events the Bible describes are what some scholars call "language events", brought to us only through words; and it is the words themselves that have the authority, not the events they describe'.[6] I do not, of course, deny the presence of story in the Bible (Jonah, Daniel, and so on). But the life, death and resurrection of Jesus is not just a tale, however evocative, but a wonderful fusion of the power of myth and the power of actuality. Nor do I deny the problems presented by the task of historical assessment. The endeavour calls for scrupulosity and delicacy of judgement, though I think that many modern scholars have greatly exaggerated the degree of difficulty involved to the point of claiming it to be virtually impossible. This is not the place to attempt to present my own conclusions from looking into the matter,[7] but I simply record that I believe, in particular, that the New Testament can be used as an evidential basis for supporting the claims of the Christian faith about its Founder, Jesus Christ.[8]

The Old Testament presents us with greater problems. Yet,

not only is the absorbing account of intrigue at the court of King David (2 Samuel 11-1 Kings 2) an extremely early example of detailed historical writing (probably antedating Herodotus by at least four centuries), but I believe that behind the multi-layered story of the foundational experience of the Exodus lies the historical reminiscence of a great act of deliverance.

Of course, the bare events themselves are not enough. Even the empty tomb (Matthew 28.5-7; Mark 16.6; Luke 24.5-7; John 20.4-9) and the resurrection itself (Matthew 28.16-20; Luke 24.38-49; John 20.19-23) need interpretation. As in science, so in theology, experience and interpretation intertwine. John Barton writes that:

> there are exceedingly few events recorded in Scripture which are crucial in that sense to Christian faith. The Bible is historical evidence in a much wider sense than this; evidence not simply to particular events, but to the whole world into which Jesus came... Scripture is most importantly a witness to the belief system of Judaism and early Christianity, within which his meaning and role can be understood.[9]

Hence the importance of what are the earliest New Testament writings, the Pauline epistles. They tell us little about the history of Jesus but a great deal about the understanding and testimony of the early Church that in him it had found new and transforming life. The Gospels were not written just to convey biographical information about Jesus (crucified on 14 Nisan, AD 33,[10] etc) but 'that you may believe that Jesus is the Christ, the Son of God, and that believing you may have life in his name' (John 20.31). A second consequence of the Christian claims is that the Bible is not just there for our detached perusal, but as the vehicle of a personal encounter, demanding a response. We are invited to commit ourselves to sharing in that experience of the first Christians that 'if anyone is in Christ he is a new creation; the old has passed away, behold, the new has come' (2 Corinthians 5.18).

That remark about our sharing with first-century Christians highlights a difficulty that many feel today about the use of the Bible. Its world is so different from our world, its thoughts from our thoughts. Then people lived in a three-decker universe and saw disease as demon possession; now we live in a universe described by big bang cosmology, and disease is seen as biochemical malfunction. How can there be kinship and communication across so great a cultural chasm? Has not much of the Bible simply sunk below our intellectual horizon? Such a view has been expressed within the Church as well as outside it.[11]

Of course there are problems here, but they are easily exaggerated. We do not think that a seed 'dies' when it is planted, but that does not affect our ability to see what Jesus in John's Gospel (John 12.24) and Paul (1 Corinthians 15.36) are getting at when they use that image. It surely cannot be central to the Christian faith to believe that Mark 5.1-20 (the story of the Garadene swine) is literally an account of an exorcism by which a legion of demons was transferred into a herd of pigs, rather than its being a report, in the idiom of its time, of a remarkable healing encounter between Jesus and a man greatly deranged.

Above all, it seems clear to me, as a matter of experienced fact, that the Bible, despite all its cultural strangeness and scientific inadequacy, does actually succeed in speaking to us across the centuries. Moreover, this engagement with another thought world can be liberating, in that it points us away from the limitations of a merely twentieth-century world-view. It would be an act of intellectual arrogance to suppose that our insight is in every respect superior to that of preceding generations. They may well have known things now forgotten or grown dim, not least in the realm of spiritual experience. Just as with our contemporaries there is 'the perfectly rational enterprise of using the wider resources of the community to extend one's own, and necessarily limited, experience and expertise',[12] so we can carry that procedure further still in our dialogue with those who are our predecessors. Such contact is, in any case, essential in order that we may recognize the womb that gave us birth. Christians are not called to practise a false antiquarianism, as if belief required an anachronistic attempt to become a first-century Palestinian, but they have to be in touch with the foundations of their faith, 'the apostles and prophets, Christ Jesus himself being the cornerstone' (Ephesians 2.20). We must be in contact with our origin. Here is a great contrast with science. I do not need to read Clerk Maxwell's classic work, the *Treatise on Electricity and Magnetism*, in order to make use of his equations. I do need to read the Gospels if I am to reckon with Christ.

'We can, without attempting to get "outside" our world, at least seek to extend our horizons.' The remark is Nicholas Lash's. He goes on to say:

> The possibility of our doing so is grounded in the fact that we are not simply 'on our own'. Each individual, each generation, is shaped by the tradition which precedes and constitutes it. Memory may play tricks, and our attempts to 'read'

the traces of the past are not without difficulty. Nevertheless, 'absolute relativism', elevating such difficulty into a metaphysical principle, is simply loss of nerve disguised as philosophy.[13]

Such loss of nerve would be particularly crippling for the Christian tradition, which must maintain its encounter with fundamental events in Israel and in the coming of Jesus Christ.

The ability of literature to speak with meaning across the centuries is a phenomenon familiar to us and by no means confined to Scripture. We encounter it in Shakespeare and the Greek tragedians. It is one of the principal arguments for a continuity of human nature lying beneath the bewildering varieties of cultural change. It is expressed in the idea of the classic, which Schlegel spoke of as 'a writing which is never fully understood. But those that are educated and educate themselves must always want to learn from it'.[14] There is a close connection between this inexhaustible character of the classic and the unlimited open fruitfulness of symbol (see Chapter 2). The universality of the classic means that it is never the possession of a sect, for it cannot be confined within narrow limits. David Tracy speaks of the classic as 'always public, never private', and he goes on to say that in the classic 'we recognize nothing less than the disclosure of a reality we cannot but name truth'.[15] The classic maintains an equipoise between then and now; it is fruitful of novelty without denying its origin in the past. As John Barton says, 'it remains itself, yet has something fresh to say to each new inquirer'.[16]

When we think of the Bible as being the supreme Christian classic, we are encouraged to read it in a particular way. I have spoken of its evidential role. In that historical mode, our reading must be critical and analytical; a concern with questions of sources and authenticity is paramount. The writing is being submitted to our evaluation. When we read Scripture in a classic mode we are submitting ourselves to it. Those of us who use the Bible in our spiritual life are engaged with the text in a way that allows it to become part of us, forming the fabric of our thought. We are experiencing its power to be the vehicle used by the Spirit to bring God's grace to us. Our concern is not then analytical, dividing the text into fragments of differing kinds and qualities, but with the totality of what is set before us. David Tracy says that 'explicitly religious classic expressions will involve a claim to truth by *the power of the whole* – as in some sense a radical and finally gracious mystery'[17] That will be true of the literary corpus of the Bible as well as of the world-view of Christian faith. The recognition that this is so is one of the central tenets of recent 'canonical criticism'[18] encouraging us to take seriously the whole and final form of Scripture. Of course the Old Testament is a combination, often within the same book, of material from different centuries, so that Yahweh is sometimes spoken of parochially as Israel's God and sometimes universally as the God of all the Earth; of course there are distressing harshnesses in tales of genocide and stoning to death, and in the vindictiveness of the cursing psalms, which mean that they cannot be taken as Christian exemplars; of course there are contrasting points of view in the New Testament (compare the attitudes of Romans 13 and Revelation 13 to the governing authorities or, more centrally, the differing approaches to Christology found in John, Paul and the Writer to the Hebrews);[19] but the bewildering richness and conflict of life is present in this sometimes dissonant diversity making up the Bible, and beneath it all, as its ground bass and unifying principle, is continuing testimony to the steadfast love of God and his Christ.

The presence of clash and contradiction within the Bible is fatal to the theory of using it as a divinely-guaranteed textbook. Those who attempt to do so either construct a tacit canon within the canon, omitting what is awkward and unseemly, or they are driven to frustration or crazy ingenuity in trying to reconcile the irreconcilable, to square the God of love with the command to Saul utterly to destroy the Amalekites (1 Samuel 15). If the reading of Scripture is to be truly edifying it will have to be in some other mode than this. The clue lies, I believe, in the assimilation of our engagement with the Bible to our fundamental experience of open engagement with symbol (see Chapter 2). 'The Biblical text mediates not information or opinion but encounter.'[20] Symbol is not to be reduced to sign by an insistence that it carry a single univocal meaning. Equally the Bible is not to be tied down; it must be acknowledged as being polysemous, having multi-layered meaning, capable of mediating many messages to its readers. John Barton tells us that 'the semantic indeterminacy of sacred texts'[21] is a continuing theme of his book, which sets out to discuss the nature of 'the authority of the Bible in Christianity'. Time and again we see this verbal fruitfulness blossoming within Scripture itself. Flattering (or reassuring) words are spoken at the coronation of a king of Judah: 'The Lord has sworn and has not changed his mind, "You are a priest for ever after the order of Melchizedek" ' (Psalm 110.4) In the mind of the Writer to the Hebrews these words trigger the sustained meditation on the eternal and effective priesthood of Christ, which is the central theme of his epistle. Melchizedek himself, a shadowy but

67

impressive figure from patriarchal history (Genesis 14), becomes the type of Christ, 'the source of eternal salvation to all who obey him' (Hebrews 5.9). A contemporary commemoration of some unknown righteous sufferer in the period of the Exile, or conceivably of the exiled community itself (Isaiah 53), provides the first Christians with the key to understanding the paradox of a crucified Messiah. The author's particular original intention is not the only meaning to be found in the words used, and the etymological fallacy (that original sense is the true sense) is no more to be imposed on passages than it is on individual words. In the biblical examples cited, there is an appropriateness of development by which intuitions of priesthood, and of the redemptive character of vicarious suffering, find their focus and fulfilment in Christ. 'Types and shadows have their ending.' This process of conceptual development does not stop with the end of the New Testament era. The Fathers recognized the varieties of meaning to be found in Scripture – the literal, the moral, and the spiritual, the last two often uncovered using methods either allegorical or typological[22] – even if some of their exegesis may seem to us to be either mechanical or fantastic. Polysemy is an indispensable element in the inexhaustible freshness of the religious classic, the Bible. Northrop Frye says of polysemous meaning, that as we read 'the feeling is approximately "there is more to be got out of this" '.[23] The process is not one of wilful imposition but of sympathetic exploration. Frye emphasizes continuity of development. 'What is implied is a single process growing in subtlety and comprehensiveness, not different senses, but different intensities of a continuous sense, unfolding like a plant out of a seed.'[24] It is this naturalness that we often feel to be missing in the allegorical extravagances of interpreters like Origen. The overplus of meaning is surely to be sought without undue strain. Yet, despite the inevitable oddities of individual expositors, the evolving tradition of the Church provides a context of the kind of continuously developing exploration to which Frye refers. It is the setting within which those of us who believe in the guidance of the Spirit will wish to pursue our own use of Scripture, not in slavish deference to the past but in the recognition that we need to profit from its insights.

If the propositional-cognitive view of theology were correct, then an account of the Bible as a divinely-guaranteed textbook of such propositions would make sense. If the cultural-linguistic view of theology were correct, then an account of the Bible as the storybook of the Christian community would make sense. In Chapter 1, I rejected both of these pictures of the nature of rational discussion in theology, proposing in their stead a criti-cal-realist view, based on an analogy with science's approach to exploring the way things are. Because it is realist, theology will want to retain an evidential appeal to Scripture as ground for belief. Because it is a critical realism, theology will seek to respect the nature of the Reality it encounters.[25] In Chapter 2, I argued that this need calls for the openness of symbol as providing the pre-ferred language of theological discourse. In the written pages of the Bible this symbolic character is realized through the polysemous nature of the literary classic.

If that understanding is correct, our use of Scripture must conform to it. The Bible provides us with indispensable access to the history of Israel's interaction with God, to the figure of Jesus Christ, and to the experience of those followers who first confessed him as Lord. We are concerned, not just with events, but with those powerful symbolic images which convey the mean-ing of what was happening in those events. Commenting on 1 Corinthians 1.18-19: 'For the word of the cross is folly to those who are perishing, but to us who are saved it is the power of God. For it is written "I will destroy the wisdom of the wise and the cleverness of the clever I will thwart" ', John Barton says that 'Scripture is here providing Paul with his vocabulary, not with prophecies looking for fulfilment'.[26] Concerning the importance of symbolic vocabulary, Austin Farrer wrote: 'The appearance of a new religion and the transformation of basic images are not simply connected things; they are one and the same thing'.[27] As we open ourselves to the symbolic richness of Scripture, we are donning those 'spectacles behind the eyes' which will enable us to view the world from a Christian perspective. There are, of course, other encounters which immerse us in Christian experi-ence. One is contact with fellow believers - here and now in the local church, over space and time in the tradition of the Great Church. Above all there is the encounter with the Lord himself in private prayer and public worship, particularly the Eucharist. Our personal use of Scripture will surely find room for that slow, meditative, dissolving reading which in the Middle Ages was called *lectio divina*. In public Christian worship the Scriptures have always had a prominent place. Nothing makes clearer the nature of their symbolic worth. People do not go to a Service of Lessons and Carols at Christmas to gain fresh information, but to allow the old familiar story to soak into them once more. The Bible finds a properly honoured place in the worshipping and obedient life of the people of God.

We need to remember that 'The books that are reckoned as

holy Scripture are intimately related to faith, indispensable for it, yet not coterminous with it'.[28] The context for the true use of Scripture is that of Christian discipleship, as we submit ourselves to the power of its divinely inspired imagery and ponder its account of divine action in history. Thus it is that the Bible is freed to make its peculiar quality felt. 'Only if it is recognized that authority does not lie solely with the Bible can the Bible achieve the authority which properly belongs to it.'[29]

What has the Bible to say to those who seek to use it in this way in order to cast light on the relationship between science and theology? The opening passages of three of the writings of the New Testament set before us the image of the Cosmic Christ: the Word (much more than rational principle but surely including the idea of such a principle) without whom 'was not anything made that was made' (John 1.3); the One of whom it can be said 'all things were created through him and for him. He is before all things and in him all things hold together' (Colossians 1.16-17); the One 'through whom also [God] created the world' (Hebrews 1.2). What greater encouragement could there be for the scientific exploration of the rational structure of the physical world, what clearer indication of its value?

In an astonishing passage in Romans, Paul extends to all creation the hope of an eventual liberty in Christ:

> For the creation waits with eager longing for the revelation of the sons of God; for the creation was subjected to futility, not of its own will but by the will of him who subjected it in hope; because the creation itself will be set free from its bondage to decay and obtain the glorious liberty of the children of God. We know that the whole creation has been groaning in travail together until now; and not only the creation, but we ourselves, who have the first fruits of the Spirit, groan inwardly as we wait for adoption as sons, the redemption of our bodies. (Romans 8.19-23)

Here is set before us no narrow anthropocentric hope but one of literally universal proportions. Earlier Paul had affirmed that something can be known of God from the inspection of the world 'namely his eternal power and deity' (Romans 1.19), a significant encouragement to pursue the insights of natural theology.

The New Testament, written by city dwellers, has comparatively little to say about nature itself, though Jesus uses natural imagery in sayings and parables. It is the Old Testament which provides many detailed appeals to the world we inhabit. They are particularly to be found in the Wisdom literature – that cool look at the way things are, which I have suggested is the form that natural theology takes in the Hebrew Scriptures and which is the nearest that Israel got to anything remotely approaching science.[30] Most striking of all such passages is the answer to Job (Job 38-41). The voice from the whirlwind, addressing that righteous sufferer, speaks mainly of an appeal to the power and mystery and 'otherness' of created nature. 'Where were you when I laid the foundations of the earth? Tell me if you have understanding' (Job 38.4). Once again there is a corrective to narrow anthropocentrism; a strong sense of God's varied purposes for all his creation pervades the discourse. The psalms frequently celebrate God's power as Creator, and the fruitfulness of his creation (Psalms 8, 19, 29, 33, 65, 96, 104, 135, 136, 139, 147), not in a sentimental way but in one which recognizes the destructiveness of the stormwind and that 'the young lions roar for their prey, seeking their food from God' (Psalm 104.21). The Hebrew mind is always aware of the threat posed by the waters of chaos, held in restraint by God alone (e.g. Psalm 93.3-4). Anyone constructing a service on a scientifically oriented theme will find much more choice of material in the psalter than in the hymnbook.

The dominant image is the value of creation and the power of its Creator, providing further encouragement to scientific exploration. A similar theme recurs in the prophetic writing most concerned with these matters, Second Isaiah. God is the ground of all that is: 'For thus says the Lord who created the heavens (he is God!), who formed the earth and made it (he established it; he did not create a chaos, he formed it to be inhabited!), "I am the Lord, and there is no other"' (Isaiah 45.18). He is no deistic God content with what he has done, but he is active, his care continues: 'Behold, the former things have come to pass, and new things I declare; before they spring forth I tell you of them' (Isaiah 42.9). God's world is one of dynamic becoming, not static being (as science has indeed discovered it to be). The comparison with the endlessly cyclic nature-religions of Canaan and Babylon, and the perpetual status quo of Egypt, is very striking.

I have left till last what many believe to be the *locus classicus* of the interaction of science and Scripture, the opening chapters of Genesis. Seldom does one give a talk about science-and-religion to a general audience without being asked how these chapters come into it. Nothing indicates more clearly than they do the need to use Scripture aright. Part of our respect for the Bible must involve our attempting to read the different parts of it in the appropriate fashion. It is a disastrous mistake to read poetry as if it were prose. 'My love is like a red, red rose' does not mean that I am in love with Ena Harkness! Nowhere is the textbook approach to Scripture more out of place than in Genesis 1-3. We are alerted to this fact by noting that two different creation stories have been juxtaposed to each other, an early account (Genesis 2.4-24) and a later one of considerable sophistication[31] (Genesis 1.1-2.3). When Genesis reached its canonical form, the redactor did not feel it necessary to conflate or reconcile these stories, as if they had been literal accounts which must be squared with each other. That in itself tells us something of how they are to be used. We read them as powerful symbolic stories (myths) conveying the idea of a total dependence of the creation upon its Creator and (most astonishing of all) the sevenfold reiterated message that all is 'good'. Science, in making untenable a literal reading of Genesis 1 and 2 (itself a tendency originating in late medieval and reformation times), has liberated these chapters to play their proper and powerful role in Christian thought.

In a similar way, Genesis 3 is to be understood as a myth about human alienation from God, and not the aetiological explanation of the only too evident plight of humanity. Science can discern no radical rift in the course of cosmic history, brought about by primeval human error. Theology can discern the truth that the root of sin is the refusal to accept the status of a creature, to seek on the contrary 'to be like God' (Genesis 3.5). Jesus is the second Adam (Romans 5.12-17; 1 Corinthians 15.22), not as the reversal of some genealogical entanglement, but because his death and resurrection restore to us the way back to the God from whom we have wandered, and they are the initiating events of God's new creation. I believe that the correct use of Scripture not only delivers us from the tortuous trickery of 'creation science' but also encourages us to find in the opening chapters of the Bible a profound source of spiritual challenge and illumination.

Exegetes differ about whether Genesis 1.1-3 presents a picture of God creating order out of primeval chaos (the *tohu wabohu*, 'without form and void', of verse 2), or whether it can be seen as pointing to the later Christian doctrine of *creatio ex nihilo*. The earliest unequivocal statement of the idea of creation out of nothing is in the apocryphal Second Book of Maccabees (2 Maccabees 7.28), but the emphasis in Genesis 1 on the dependence of all upon the sovereign will of God for its existence ('And God said "Let there be..."') is certainly consonant with the central significance of *creatio ex nihilo*. Many modern theological writers wish to combine that emphasis on creaturely ontological dependence with a notion of *creatio continua*, God's unfolding purposive action through the evolving history of the universe.[32] That sits somewhat uneasily with the 'seventh day' of sabbath rest (Genesis 2.1-3), with its implication of the completed work of creation, though some ingenious commentators suggest that cosmic sabbath is yet to come. Continuing creation is, of course, perfectly consonant with the talk of God's new things which we find in Second Isaiah. A discriminating use of biblical imagery is surely legitimate for us as we seek to integrate what we learn from the book of Scripture with what we learn from the book of nature. Such discrimination is part of the proper use of Scripture.

6 Cross-Traffic

Our discussion so far has been concerned with drawing certain analogies between the procedures of science and theology and proposing that both should be located within a common framework of the rational investigation of reality. Our concern has been more with style than content. It is now time to consider what cross-traffic there may be between the disciplines in terms of their actual descriptions of the world.

I write from within the Western Christian tradition. That tradition's approach to the physical world has been characterized by a commitment to reality, a search for rationality, and an acknowledgement of contingency. It has been argued,[1] with some plausibility in my view, that just such an ideological setting was the necessary matrix for the development of modern science, thus making it intelligible why science first arose in Europe (rather than, say, China).

Theologically, the reality of the physical world and the value set upon investigating it derive from the doctrine that it is God's creation. That world's rational structure, apprehended by science, is taken to be an expression of the Mind of its Creator. I shall return to that issue later. Theologically, the contingency of the world is a reflection of God's freedom to create whatever he wills. For science it implies the necessity of experiment and observation: we have to look and see how things actually are. A similar necessity is placed upon theology, with the implication, *inter alia*, that it must listen to what science has to say. The theologian cannot discourse on the doctrine of creation without condescending to pay attention to what is actually found written in the Book of Nature. In both disciplines, as their histories show, we must be prepared for surprises. Our power of rational prevision is strictly limited.

What then is the mutual relationship of science and theology? Each has its own decent degree of autonomy. We have every reason to believe that scientifically posable questions will prove to be scientifically answerable. In that sense, science requires no assistance from theology. To suppose the contrary would be to fall into the error of the God of the gaps. Equally, theology is concerned with its own phenomena (in essence, the experience of the presence of God) and the understanding of them. Science, because of its self-defining limitation to a restricted class of generalizable, largely impersonal, occurrences (a restriction itself the very enabler of science's success) is in no position to endorse or deny the claims of religion. To suppose the contrary would be to fall into the error of scientism. Yet the two disciplines are not completely separable. There is an inescapable degree of interaction between their world-views, but one which is not symmetrical in form across the boundary. The asymmetry arises from the nature of theology. To be concerned with questions of God is to be concerned with the totality of all that is real. Necessarily, theology must take account of the deliverances of all the varieties of human inquiry, whether they be those of science into the physical world, or aesthetics into beauty, or ethics into goodness, or its own 'particular' domain of revelatory encounter with the divine. I have written elsewhere of theology that:

> If it is to lay claim to its medieval title of the Queen of the Sciences that will not be because it is in a position to prescribe the answers to questions discussed by other disciplines. Rather it will be because it must avail itself of their answers in the conduct of its own inquiry, thereby setting them within the most profound context available. Theology's regal status lies in its commitment to seek the deepest possible level of understanding.[2]

What theology can do for science is to provide answers to those meta-questions which arise from science but which are not themselves scientific in character. The role of theology as providing the ultimate quenching of the thirst for an understanding through and through is one which has been particularly stressed in the tradition stemming from Thomas Aquinas. A twentieth-century Thomist thinker, Bernard Lonergan, wrote of God as 'the unrestricted act of understanding, the eternal rapture glimpsed in every Archimedean cry of Eureka'.[3]

What science can do for theology is to tell it what the physical world is actually like. In so doing it imposes conditions of consonance which the broader considerations of theology must respect. The doctrine of creation has to respond to the fact that the history of the universe is one of simplicity evolving into complexity over billions of years, rather than the springing-into-being of a ready-made world a few thousand years ago. That will surely encourage thought of a Creator who is patient and subtle in his operation. The need for consonance with the findings of science can be a healthy corrective for theology, whose persistent temptation is to indulge in ungrounded speculation.

I want to illustrate these general observations by giving two answers to meta-questions (theology's gifts to science) and three examples of the constraining demands of consonance (science's gifts to theology), taken largely from the experience of contemporary physics. We will start with the former.

(a) *Intelligibility* One of the most striking features of the physical world is its rational transparency to us. We have come to take it for granted that we can understand the universe, but it is surely a highly significant fact about it that this is the case. Einstein once said that the only incomprehensible thing about the universe is that it is comprehensible. He was referring to what Eugene Wigner, in a memorable phrase, called 'the unreasonable effectiveness of mathematics'.[4] Time and again we have found that the physical theories which fit the facts are characterized in their formulation by the unmistakable quality of mathematical beauty. It is an actual technique in fundamental physics to seek theories endowed with mathematical economy and elegance, in the (historically justified) expectation that they will be the ones which describe the way the world actually is. There is a marvellous congruence between the workings of our minds (the mathematical reason within) and the workings of the physical world (the scientific reason without). Of course, up to a point the need to survive in the evolutionary struggle provides an explanation of why this is so. If our thoughts did not match in some degree the world around us we should all have perished. But that can only apply to the relation of everyday experience (the world of rocks and trees) to everyday thinking (counting and Euclidean geometry). Wigner was not talking about anything as banal as that. He had in mind such things as the counterintuitive quantum world, whose strangeness is made sense of in terms of highly abstract mathematical entities. It is hard to believe that the ability to conceive of quantum field theory is just a spin-off from evolutionary competition.

Science does not explain the mathematical intelligibility of the physical world, for it is part of science's founding faith that this is so. Of course, we can always decline to put the question, shrug our shoulders and say 'That's the way it is, and good luck for you mathematical chaps'. It goes against the grain for a scientist to be so intellectually supine. The meta-question of the unreasonable effectiveness of mathematics insists on being answered. A coherent and elegant explanation would lie in the theological claim that the reason within and the reason without are linked together by their common origin in the Rationality of the Creator. The physical universe seems shot through with signs of mind. That is indeed so, says the theist, for it is God's Mind that lies behind its rational beauty. I do not offer this as a knockdown argument for theism – there are no such arguments, either for or against – but as a satisfying insight which finds a consistent place in a theistic view of the world.

(b) *The Anthropic Principle* I shall not once again rehearse the many considerations that have led people to the conclusion that a physical world which is fruitful in evolving complexity out of simplicity, to the degree that an almost homogeneous ball of energy becomes, after fifteen billion years, a home for self-conscious beings, is not in scientific terms 'any old world', but rather one which is very special in the finely-tuned balance of its law and circumstance.[5] Notice that we are referring here, not to particular occurrences within cosmic history, but to those natural laws which are the necessary ground of all such occurrence. These laws contain certain parameters specifying the intrinsic strengths of the forces of nature. The laws take particular forms - in our universe they are quantum mechanical and, more specifically, they appear to correspond to spontaneously broken gauge theories. There are also certain givens about our universe itself (its size, for instance) which play an important part in determining its history. The Anthropic Principle suggests that quite small variations in any of these fundamental specifications of our world would have rendered it anthropically sterile. They would have condemned it to a boringly unproductive history.

It is important to emphasize that these delicate balances needed for anthropic fruitfulness are required at all stages of cosmic process. They do not refer only to the earliest instants (getting off to a good start, a world neither too dilute nor threatened with premature collapse), but also to its continuing history (the formation of main sequence stars, needed to synthesize the heavier elements, must be possible and some of them must explode as supernovae so that the building blocks of life become available for subsequent use) and to its detailed process (for instance, the chemistry of carbon and the properties of water). Significant 'coincidences' in given law and circumstance appear to be necessary at every stage of the world's development if that history is to prove capable of fertility.

If we accept this view, then a meta-question arises of why things are this way. That seems to me to be the interesting form of inquiry, stronger in intent than the 'Weak Anthropic Principle' (which simply observes that our presence in the universe necessarily imposes certain constraints of consistency, which require its circumstances to be compatible with that fact), and not as scientifically pretentious as the 'Strong Anthropic Principle' (which purports to claim that the universe must be such that observers arise within it).[6] Instead one has what one might call the 'Moderate Anthropic Principle', which notes the contingent fruitfulness of the universe as being a fact of interest calling for an explanation. Of course, if things were not that way we would not be here to worry about them, but it does not seem enough just to say 'We're here because we're here' and leave it at that. Instead there is the hint of an amazing anti-Copernican revolution. We don't live at the centre of the universe, but it does look as though the very fabric of the cosmos has been given a character which is required if the emergence of beings like us is to be a possibility. There seems to be the chance of a revised and revived argument from design – not appealing to Paley's Cosmic Craftsman working within physical process (which process science explains in a way not requiring intervention by such a God of the gaps) – but appealing to a Cosmic Planner who has endowed his world with a potentiality implanted within the delicate balance of the laws of nature themselves (which laws science cannot explain since it *assumes* them as the basis for its explanation of the process). In short, the claim would be that the universe is indeed not 'any old world' but the carefully calculated construct of its Creator. The Strong Anthropic Principle is then seen to be an intuition of teleological truth, but of a theological rather than scientific character.

It is necessary to consider a number of arguments advanced in rebuttal of such a claim:

(i) Perhaps there is in fact only one possible world; that it is an illusion that things could have been different. Perhaps the strengths of the fundamental forces have to be just what they are for reasons of consistency. [A more sophisticated version would say that there are different cosmic domains of symmetry breaking in which the force ratios take different values, but if there are enough such domains then one of them will be within anthropic limits, and that's where we live because we couldn't turn up anywhere else.] Such claims of a rational inevitability in the way things are have recently had some fluctuating degree of popularity among physicists. They spring from the difficulties encountered in fully reconciling quantum theory and general relativity, with the consequent speculation that there might essentially be only one way in which to do so. But even if that proves to be the case, we have already built in powerful tacit specifications of the worlds that we are prepared to talk about. They have to be quantum mechanical, contain Einsteinian gravity, and so on. I see no reason why among possible worlds there should not be a Newtonian world, made up of billiard ball atoms and with gravitational action-at-a-distance, or a world without gravity altogether and consisting of just electrons and photons. For sure, they would not be anthropically fruitful worlds, but that's what we are discussing. I don't think the uniqueness argument stands up. Even if it did, it would surely be rather remarkable that the only possible universe was a fruitful one.

(ii) At the other extreme, perhaps, there are lots and lots of different universes, each with its own law and circumstance and existing independently of each other. In that case, it would be no more surprising that one of them fulfilled the anthropic condition than it would be to find an almost spherical pebble if one had sorted over a million specimens in the first place. Once again it would be that particular universe that we live in because we couldn't turn up anywhere else. This 'portfolio of universes' approach has been quite popular in one way or another. It can be tricked out in various scientific-sounding ways (by *illegitimate* invocation of many-worlds quantum theory,[7] or by speculations about vacuum fluctuations of ur-stuff, for instance) but it seems to me not to be a scientific proposal at all (for scientifically we only have adequate motivation to speak of this particular universe of our actual physical experience). Rather it is a metaphysical guess. Its interest lies in the fact that by making such guesses people indicate clearly that they feel there is really something calling for an explanation. To my mind a metaphysical speculation of equal coherence and greater economy is that there is just one universe, anthropically finely-tuned because it is the creation of a Creator who wills it to be capable of fruitful purpose. Again, I present that as a proffered insight, not a knockdown argument.

(iii) The most interesting counter-argument is that the Anthropic Principle is the fruit of limited imagination, for its questions of balance centre around the conditions necessary to ensure the eventual development of a carbon-based life. Perhaps intelligence and self-consciousness could have totally different embodiments, not based on carbon chemistry – a thinking plasma maybe. Perhaps all universes (or a great many) are capable of producing their own idiosyncratic forms of 'life'? Perhaps... But those who speak this way are drawing a very large intellectual blank cheque on an unknown account. The only form of intelligent and self-conscious life that we know about is carbon-based. When one considers the physical complexity of the human brain (far and away the most intricately interconnected physical system we have ever encountered), it is difficult not to believe that this degree of structure is necessary as the physical substrate

79

sustaining self-consciousness, and it is very hard to believe that there are many radically different ways of realizing naturally such a necessary complexity. Our knowledge of how brain and mind relate is so pitifully rudimentary that no one can be dogmatic about what is possible, but I regard it as wholly reasonable not to entertain seriously this ground for rebutting the claim of anthropic significance.

Having said all that, I do not doubt that some anthropic 'coincidences' which now seem special may be found to result from other, deeper, linkages. [So-called inflationary cosmology – the primeval boiling of space – has already provided one possible example of how this might happen, in relation to the anthropic requirement that cosmic expansion and gravitational attraction must be very evenly balanced in a fruitful universe, which must neither become too dilute nor suffer too prompt collapse.] However, I think it is reasonable to expect that there will still be some things distinctly and minutely particular about a world capable of producing men and women. I therefore conclude that there is indeed a meta-question arising from Anthropic Principle considerations to which theism provides a persuasive (but not logically coercive) answer.

Let us now consider three constraints of consonance which science might seem to lay upon theological thought:

(a) *Origins* Perhaps no subject has given rise to more confusion in the interrelationship of science and theology than the question of how things began. It has often erroneously been supposed that the Christian doctrine of creation is principally concerned with initiation, with the primary instant. To think that is to confuse Christianity with deism. The doctrine of creation is concerned, not just with what God did, but with what he is doing; its subject is ontological origin, not temporal beginning. Its central assertion is that the physical world, at every instant of its existence, is held in being by the will of God. Two consequences follow. The first is that, if physical cosmology delivers us a dateable moment when the universe as we know it sprang forth from the Big Bang, that is scientifically very interesting but theologically neutral. There never was a theological stake in preferring big bang cosmology to steady state cosmology. Secondly, and conversely, if physical cosmology were to abolish a dateable beginning for the world, no great theological upheaval would follow. Stephen Hawking has proposed a highly speculative, but just conceivably correct, quantum cosmology in which the universe is a kind of fuzzy spacetime egg with no sharp beginning. He says 'If the universe is really completely self-contained, having no boundary or edge, it would have neither beginning nor end; it would simply be. What place then for a creator?'[8] It is theologically naive to give any other answer than 'every place' – as the ordainer and sustainer of the spacetime egg. God is not a God of the Edges, with a vested interest in boundaries. In fact there is a contemporary current of thought in theology, particularly associated with Jürgen Moltmann,[9] which stresses the gift of a genuine 'otherness' made by a loving Creator to his creation, and which would find very consonant physical realization in a universe 'really completely self-contained'. If there are problems for Christian theology in cosmological thought they lie, not in questions of origins, but in the question of:

(b) *The End* Cosmologists not only peer into the past but they can also attempt to descry the future. On the grandest scale, cosmic history is a tug of war between two opposing principles: the explosion of the big bang, throwing matter apart, and the pull of gravity, drawing matter together. They are very evenly balanced and we do not know which will win. Accordingly, we have to consider two alternative scenarios for the universe's future. If expansion wins, the galaxies will continue to fly apart for ever. Within themselves gravity will certainly win and they will condense into gigantic black holes, eventually decaying into low-grade radiation. That way lies cosmic death. The alternative scenario presents no more cheerful a prospect. If gravity wins, the present expansion will one day be halted and reversed. What began with the Big Bang will end with the Big Crunch, as the universe falls back into a singular cosmic melting pot. That way lies collapse.

On the face of it, the ultimate prospects are bleak. What does that imply for theology's claim that there is a purpose at work in the world? Christian orthodoxy has never subscribed to an evolutionary optimism which expects a total fulfilment of divine will to be brought about within the flux of present physical process. If there is a true and lasting hope – and it is a deep human intuition that there is such a hope – then it can only rest in the eternal mercy and faithfulness of God himself. Christians believe that for themselves (our bodies will decay on a time scale of tens of years) in their assertion of a destiny beyond death, and they can believe it as well for the whole universe (whose decay will be on a time scale of tens of billions of years). We need to embrace a cosmic hope as well as a personal hope, for it would be far too anthropocentric simply to regard this vast universe as being of concern to God only as the backdrop for a human drama which has just started after an overture lasting fifteen billion years.[10] It is, of course, beyond our feeble powers of imagination to conceive what that act of cosmic redemption will be like, but if there is a true hope it lies in God and not in physics.

Some of those unable to embrace a hope arising from casting oneself on divine faithfulness have engaged in ingenious speculation about whether there might nevertheless be some form of adequate fulfilment attainable within physical process. As cosmic circumstances change radically within the universe's evolving history, the embodiment of intelligence would have to adapt itself to what is going on. Carbon-based life would have to give way to successors which it had itself produced by conscious design. There might eventually indeed be 'thinking plasmas', engineered by their predecessors in the great chain of intelligent being. In this way, even within the chronologically finite history of a collapsing universe, there could be such rapidly accelerating processing of information that a kind of infinite 'psychological' history would be able to unfold, and even within the infinitely drawn-out dying gasp of a decaying universe, ever-slowing but continuing process might achieve a comparable fulfilment. This kind of 'physical eschatology' has been pursued particularly by Freeman Dyson[11] and Frank Tipler[12]. Tipler exhibits great speculative ingenuity, even to the point of supposing that as embodied intelligence approached its ultimate phase (which he calls Omega and equates with a kind of physical realization of God) it could recover traces of our past lives and reconstitute isomorphic models of ourselves in a final act of 'resurrection'. Yet it seems to me that it is an etiolated and abstractly generalized hope that his fast-racing cosmic computers would fulfil. In contrast, the Christian hope is that nothing of individual and particular good is ever lost in the Lord and that a future awaits us of unending exploration of the riches of divine reality.

(c) *Chance and Necessity* As we survey the cosmic process which has carried the world from initial simplicity to present differentiated complexity, at every stage the realization of anthropic fruitfulness has depended upon an interplay of two opposing tendencies, which we can conveniently summarize in slogan form as 'chance' and 'necessity'. By chance is meant just happenstance, the way things come together in an essentially uncorrelated sequence of occurrences: a fluctuation produces a little more primeval matter here than there; a genetic mutation produces a new characteristic of animal life. Through such novel offerings of chance there came about the condensation of the galaxies and the origin of new species. Yet, for those things to happen also requires the operation

82

of lawful necessity to preserve and sift the novelty provided: gravity enhancing the matter fluctuation; evolutionary biology operating within a stable, and so effectively selective, environment.

Some have felt that the role assigned to chance subverts religious claims of a Purpose at work. After all, what will eventually happen is not foreseeable at the beginning. The universe is given something of the air of a game of cosmic roulette. With characteristic Gallic rhetoric, Jacques Monod spoke of 'pure chance, absolutely free but blind, at the base of the stupendous edifice of evolution'.[13] For him the role of chance turned cosmic history into a tale told by an idiot, full of sound and fury, signifying nothing.

At times one feels that Monod lost sight of the indispensable, complementary, role of necessity, with its implications of finely-tuned anthropic law. If one attempts a more even-handed evaluation of the interplay of chance and necessity, then an alternative metaphysical interpretation becomes possible which is, in my view, fully consonant with Christian theology.[14]

The Christian God is both loving and faithful. The gift of the God of love to his creation will surely be freedom. He will prove to be no Cosmic Tyrant, holding all in tight control. Yet freedom by itself can only too readily degenerate into licence and chaos. The gift of the God of faithfulness will surely be reliability. He will prove to be no Cosmic Lord of Misrule. Yet reliability by itself can only too readily degenerate into an iron rigidity. We may expect the creation of the God who is both loving and faithful to display characteristics of both openness and regularity, such as are in fact reflected in the physical interplay of chance and necessity in the process of the world.

A doctrine of creation of this open yet regular kind can indeed be found in contemporary Christian theology, not only in the writings of Moltmann,[15] but also in the work of the English theologian, W. H. Vanstone. He is motivated, not by acquaintance with the scientific story, but by meditation on the necessary precariousness and value of any act of creation by love. This leads him to write 'If the creation is the work of love, then its shape cannot be predetermined by the Creator, nor its triumph foreknown: it is the realization of vision, but of vision which is discovered only through its own realization.'[16] Such an account is perfectly consonant with the scientific insight of the realization of anthropic fruitfulness through the shuffling explorations of happenstance.

This understanding can afford us some help with what is for theology the most painful of its difficulties. I refer, of course, to the problem of evil. Some modest help with the question of moral evil (the chosen cruelties of humankind) is given by the so-called free-will defence. It asserts that a world of freely choosing beings is better than a world of perfectly programmed automata, however destructive some of those choices may be. Our instinctive recoil from coercive measures such as the castration of persistent sex offenders, shows us that we accord some force to this insight. However it leaves untouched the problem of physical evil (disease and disaster). I believe this needs what I have called the 'free-process defence',[17] appealing to the divine gift of freedom to *all* of the creation, not just to human kind alone. Austin Farrer once asked himself what was God's will in the Lisbon earthquake. His answer – hard but true – was that the elements of the Earth's crust should act in accordance with their nature. God wills neither the act of a murderer nor the incidence of a cancer, but he allows both to happen in a world to which he has granted the freedom to be itself.

The greatest revision that science has had to make in its account of physical reality was brought about by the discovery of quantum theory. So counterintuitive was the subatomic world thus revealed to investigation, that the resulting understanding has been invoked in support of all kinds of metaphysical propositions, including a great variety of theological positions. This particular form of cross-traffic is sufficiently complicated and interesting to require a chapter of its own.

7 Quantum Questions

We have already had occasion several times to refer to quantum theory and its consequences for our thinking about the physical world and about questions of reality. This chapter will attempt a more systematic discussion of the issues involved. It will seek to do so in non-technical terms, but it cannot escape from being conceptually demanding. Such a necessity arises from the counter-intuitive character of the quantum world itself, which results in its discovery having caused the most radical revision of physical thinking since the start of modern science. In comparison, relativity theory – despite its abolition of absolute space and time – was no more than a profound variation on a familiar theme.[1] The physical world described by that theory remained picturable and determinate, but both these qualities disappeared with the advent of quantum mechanics. That is why Einstein was happy with his relativistic offspring but opposed to the quantum theory of which he was (through his discussion of the photoelectric effect) the regretful grandparent. He confused naive objectivity with reality, and in his defence of the latter believed he needed to reaffirm the former, thus aligning himself with the Newtonian past rather than with the future which lay with Heisenberg.

Most theologians, if they have taken account of the advent of quantum theory at all, have done so in the most generalized way. It is perhaps not too great a caricature to say that their main reaction was to feel that they detected a congenial kind of 'spiritualizing' of the gross matter of nineteenth-century materialism. John Macquarrie sums up a common attitude when he says that: 'We have already warned against any rash inference from scientific findings to philosophical generalizations, but *prima facie* one would say that the world conceived by the new physics seems more amenable – or at least less intractable – to a religious interpretation than was the world of the older physics.'[2] If that is true, I suggest it is because, by opening our eyes to enlarged possibilities, the new physics has discouraged a narrow and mechanical reductionism. The material world has certainly not been abolished – Ian Barbour judiciously comments that 'it would be as dubious to attempt to build a metaphysics of idealism on modern physics as it was to build a metaphysics of materialism on classical physics'[3] – but it has been shown to be more subtle and less particulate than our predecessors believed it to be. The interconnected and elusive character that quantum theory attributes to the physical world has been held by some to be in closer accord with the ideas of Eastern religions[4] than with the sternly realist approach of the Judaeo-Christian-Islamic tradition. I have elsewhere given my reasons for not seeing it that way.[5] In essence, my argument is that the quantum world is partially dissolving yet also structured, and this dual character corresponds more closely to the Near-Eastern balance between the nature of God in his immanence and his transcendence, encountered through the religious experiences of the mystical and the numinous. It is all too possible to exaggerate the 'looseness' of quantum mechanics. One of its early triumphs was to explain the *stability* of atoms and the *structure* of the periodic table of the elements. The wavemechanical patterns, whose weaving constitutes those atomic states, are solutions of a perfectly orderly and continuous differential equation, the Schrödinger equation. Fitfulness and discontinuity are only occasional features of the quantum world and the discrete and episodic picture of physical process presented by A. N. Whitehead's event-dominated philosophy is as much a half-truth as is the attempted assimilation of quantum theory to Eastern thought by Fritjof Capra and Gary Zukav.

It is time to descend from generalities to a more detailed account of quantum theory and its insights. At the level of the formulation of the theory it is perfectly agreed and plain wherein its revolutionary character lies. *Quantum theory permits the mixing together of what was classically immiscible.* More technically, it is based on the principle of the superposition of states.[6] In plainer terms, quantum theory not only has states in which a particle is located 'here' or it is located 'there', but it also has states which are a mixture of these two. This combination is not to be interpreted as corresponding to the particle being located in between 'here' and 'there' (for that is another kind of state altogether) but it is understood in a statistical sense as corresponding to a situation in which there are specific probabilities that on investigation the particle will be found 'here' or that on investigation it will be found 'there'. Immediately we encounter, in the most uncompromising fashion, the twin features which give quantum theory its counterintuitive character: unpicturability and a purely probabilistic interpretation.

The superposition principle illustrates one of the general effects of the discovery of quantum mechanics – that it has brought about an extension of the limits of what is conceivable. Our imaginations have been enlarged. The mixtures of which it speaks lie quite

86

outside the thought world of classical physics. They provide the basis for the consistent reconciliation of apparent opposites, which is involved in the notion of complementarity (see Chapter 2). One can see that most clearly in the way in which quantum field theory provides the formalism perfectly adapted to a duality of wave and particle. Because it concerns a field, it has the property of extension in space that goes with wavelike behaviour; because it is quantized, its energy and momentum come in the countable and indivisible packets (quanta) that go with particlelike behaviour. [It is worth permitting oneself the luxury of a technical aside to make the point more clearly. The phase operators – whose eigenvalues correspond to a specific field behaviour – do not commute with the number operators – whose eigenvalues correspond to specific numbers of particles. Consequently, a wavelike state is one with an *indefinite* number of quanta. Such a mixture of different numbers of particles present in the same state is quite unacceptable to classical physics but quite natural to quantum physics. This enhanced possibility of what can be the case enables a wave/particle type of behaviour which is simply inconceivable in classical physics.] A more homely example of wave/particle duality is provided by the analysis, fundamental to any account of quantum theory, of the double-slit experiment.[7] Quantum entities – electrons let us say – are incident upon a detecting screen after having passed through an intermediate screen pierced by two slits, separating source from detector. It is found that they arrive one by one (that is the particle aspect), but when the pattern of arrivals is analysed after many such individual detections, it is found to take the familiar form of a diffraction pattern or set of interference fringes (that is the wave aspect). This pattern occurs even if the source is so weak that at any one time only one (indivisible) electron is traversing the system. Since the appearance of the fringes depends critically upon both slits in the screen being open, one is driven to the (classically unintelligible) conclusion that the electron 'went through both slits'. (Otherwise, if it only went through one slit, whether the other was open or closed would be irrelevant – but it isn't.) What is classically nonsensical is quantum mechanically perfectly intelligible: the electron's state is a superposition of the state in which it goes through one slit with the state in which it goes through the other. The diffraction pattern on the detecting screen corresponds to the interference effects between these two components, added together to form the single wavefunction describing the electron's state. I have already emphasized (see Chapter 2) that physics is lucky enough not to have been left with two incompatible models (wave and particle) which it has to use as adroitly and cautiously as it can, to avoid contradiction. Dirac furnished it with the reconciliation of wave and particle through his invention of quantum field theory. Richard Swinburne spoke of loosening semantic rules to speak of 'wave' and 'particle' and he went on to say 'With the new analogical sense of "wave" and "particle", is it coherent to suppose light is both a stream of "particles" and a "wave"? I know of no straightforward proof that it is or that it is not.'[8] The demonstration he apparently sought in vain is provided by the quantum field theory of the electromagnetic field.

Quantum theory extends the limits of the conceivable to a quite remarkable degree, even including the limits of logic itself. One of the axioms of classical logic is the distributive law. According to this principle, if 'A is at X or Y', then either 'A is at X' or 'A is at Y'. That is not so if A is an electron. A may be in a state which is a superposition of the state (A at X) and the state (A at Y), and that is quite a different state from either of those two possibilities separately since, according to the probability interpretation, sometimes it will result in finding A at X and sometimes in finding A at Y, but we cannot tell which it will be on any particular occasion. Such a combination is a possibility undreamed of by Aristotle. He excluded any middle term between (at X) and (not at X), whilst quantum theory readily superposes these two classical incompatibles, producing (sometimes at X). The need to accommodate this extended range of options leads to the possibility of replacing classical logic by quantum logic.[9]

Strange as these ideas may seem to our notions of everyday common sense, they do not constitute the greatest surprise associated with quantum theory. I believe the latter to be the fact that more than sixty years after that theory's discovery, and despite its brilliant successes, we still cannot agree on how quantum mechanics should be interpreted. The crux of the difficulty is the *measurement problem*. In the quantum world we may combine together the possibilities of 'here' and 'there', but when we interrogate it from our macroscopic point of view, it always yields, on each occasion of inquiry, a perfectly clear and everyday answer: either 'here' or 'there', but never both. How does this come about? How does the act of measurement unscramble those superposed possibilities and plump for one of them on a particular occasion? In the jargon of the subject this perplexity is called the problem of 'the collapse of the wavefunction' – probability which was spread out over 'here', 'there' and, perhaps, 'everywhere', suddenly is focused on the actually realized result of the observation. It is somewhat humiliating for the physicist to have to confess that there is no universally agreed or wholly satisfactory answer to that reasonable question.[10] There have, however, been a number of proposals:

(i) *Determinism* The first suggestion is that there is no problem. The statistical character of quantum theory is to be attributed to our ignorance of certain effects ('hidden variables') which, when taken together with what we do know, serve completely to determine what is going on. On this view, microscopic quantum measurement is no different from classical macroscopic measurement; in each case it is simply the revealing of what was already objectively the case. It is a matter of considerable delicacy to find an empirically adequate theory with such a property – in fact, John von Neumann thought that he had proved it could not be done – but David Bohm achieved the brilliant feat of doing just that.[11] The difficulty is the way in which he did so. Bohm's theory not only has particles (which are the entities we actually observe with our detecting apparatus and which are, from this point of view, just the same as particles in classical physics) but also a wave (which encodes information about the whole environment, but whose only physical effect is to guide the motion of the particles).[12] The way in which the introduction of this somewhat ghostly wave multiplies entities is one of the reasons why Bohm's theory has not commanded much support among physicists. Other, more technical, problems relate to the equation the wave satisfies (it is the Schrödinger equation, but its adoption seems a rather *ad hoc* step, a contrivance to get the right answer); the fact that the wave is in configuration space (for a system of n particles the wave is in a space of 3n dimensions[13]); the way in which an initial probability distribution for the particles' states of motion is simply inserted; and the relation of the theory to special relativity (the problem is connected with the issues of nonlocality which we discuss below, which are particularly critical for Bohm since he attributes a clear ontological status to the wavefunction). In consequence, not many physicists feel that this is the solution to their problem.[14]

(ii) *Many-Worlds* The next suggestion is that it is all a trick of perspective. The quantum mechanical formalism (the Schrödinger equation or its equivalents) is perfectly continuous. The alleged discontinuity of wavefunction collapse, brought about by the act of measurement, is inharmoniously imposed upon this continuity as an additional postulate. Let us have none of it. Instead, let us suppose that everything that could happen does happen. It is, perhaps, a trick of my consciousness that induces me to believe that the electron was found 'here'. There is 'another me' which observed it 'there', but it is in the nature of human biography that I am unaware of that *alter ego* and his observation, incompatible with mine. In some sense, the two of us live in disjoint universes. I have phrased the proposal in terms of the impressions of a human observer. If you find that too anthropocentric, it could easily be reformulated in terms of living beings generally or in terms of the macroscopic registration of the outcome of quantum events. The essential point is that it is assumed that all possible results occur in a proliferating portfolio of parallel worlds. There is no special and unique outcome. That is the nub of Hugh Everett's many-worlds interpretation of quantum theory.[15] Michael Lockwood has protested about its being described as entailing the continual splitting of the universe into a series of parallel universes, saying 'it would be closer to the mark to say that it is the universe that splits the observer'.[16] It does not seem to me to matter much whether the ontological extravagance of this proposal is expressed globally or locally. Either way it is scarcely persuasive. The only physicists who have felt attracted in numbers to this way of thinking are the cosmologists.[17] The whole universe is a peculiar and unique kind of physical system and it is by no means obvious that it should be feasible to apply quantum theory to it, just like that. But if such a quantum cosmology were to be rightly conceived, one can see the attraction that many-worlds quantum theory would have for it. The absence of any real role for the observer in Everett's interpretation (since observers are simply cloned to accommodate the multi-faceted needs of the continuously evolving wavefunction) makes it readily adaptable for such a cosmic purpose.

(iii) *Stochastic Jumps* The third suggestion is that collapse is happening all the time, but much more frequently for large bits of measuring apparatus such as we find in the laboratory, than for isolated quantum entities. Ghirardi, Rimmer and Weber proposed a model in which spontaneous 'jumps' take place randomly, but with a frequency which depends upon the number of particles involved.[18] For an individual electron the effect is negligible (once every hundred million years, say), but once that electron is associated with a large piece of apparatus (made up of more than 10^{20} particles), collapse is virtually instantaneous. The GRW model is amusing but contrived. Its *ad hoc* character scarcely encourages the thought that it might prove the solution to the problem, but it has the merit of introducing new physics so that, in principle, it could be tested experimentally.

(iv) *Emergence Upward* The fourth suggestion is that the capacity for 'classical' measuring apparatus to be able to collapse the wavefunction is an upwardly emergent property of matter-in-organization, representing a level shift within the chain of physical complexity, comparable to the level shifts involved in the emergence of living beings and of conscious beings. (It would, of course, be possible to propose coincidence with one or other of these last level shifts, as is attempted when it is suggested that it is the intervention of a conscious observer which brings about a determinate experimental answer.) The fact that the act of measurement involves the irreversible registration of a result,[19] together with the well-known property of the laws of physics that they are reversible on a microscopic scale but (thermodynamically) irreversible on a macroscopic scale, lends some credence to this point of view. If the thermodynamic property emerges, why should not the measurement property emerge along with it? This way of thinking offers hope of producing a revised and more satisfactory version of the celebrated Copenhagen interpretation of quantum theory. The latter, in its classic statement, was more a decree than an explanation. Bohr simply laid it down that there were both quantum entities and also pieces of classical measuring apparatus which played the determining role. He sought to avoid the perplexity which would arise if one took seriously the fact that the apparatus was itself made out of quantum constituents, by asserting that the two were to be clamped together in the description of a single measuring event or 'phenomenon'. In that case, one could adroitly readjust allocations to the two halves of the phenomenon so as to avoid any overt inconsistency which might otherwise threaten if one were permitted to take the event apart and look at each half separately. (Bohr's own defence of quantum theory against the onslaughts of Einstein showed that for consistency it might be necessary to treat such a classical-looking object as the intermediate screen in the two-slits experiment, as being itself subject to quantum mechanical uncertainty.[20] In other words, one might have hastily to redraw the dividing line between the quantum and the classical to get out of a threatened contradiction.) The need for such nimbleness indicates the unresolved dualism (quantum/classical) which was so unsatisfactory a feature of Bohr's account. A revised version, seeking to overcome the arbitrary division of physical reality into two kinds of stuff, would be promising, but at present its achievement is no more than a pious hope.

(v) *Emergence Downwards* Fifthly, and finally, one might suggest that quantum theory itself was the emergent, in this case in a downward direction, as the simplified microscopic approximation to a more richly structured reality. This is the possibility which was briefly considered at the end of Chapter 3. The measurement problem is intimately connected with the operation of the superposition principle. The latter's linearity has the effect of associating with the wavefunction every possible outcome in a perfectly even-handed way – it simply adds them all together. (Technical aside: This possibly somewhat gnomic observation seeks to distil the essence of von Neumann's account of the measurement problem.) The introduction of a non-linearity, significant macroscopically but negligible microscopically, could prove capable of breaking this even-partition of possibility and so facilitate the selection of a definite result. Speculative proposals of this kind have been made by Wigner (in relation to a model for the possible downward effects of consciousness) and by Penrose (in relation to a new theory of quantum gravity – he says, highly controversially, that wavefunction collapse 'must be a quantum gravity effect')[21]. Such schemes are stimulating, but far too speculative and unsupported empirically, to be thought of as providing a conclusive solution to the problem.

The moral for theology resulting from this tangled tale of physics might be thought to be that the former is not the only subject which has difficulty in finding a consistent basis for its thinking. If our encounter with the physical world is perplexing, our encounter with the divine can scarcely be expected to yield to ready rationalization. To speak in this way is not to encourage a complacent acceptance of confused thought, but simply to acknowledge the difficulty of the task of rational inquiry. Quantum physicists must continue the search for a proper interpretation of their theory, whilst holding fast to the brilliant and successful understanding it has yielded into many aspects of physical process, from why atoms are stable to why stars shine. Similarly, theologians must seek the most coherent account of the nature of God and of his ways with humankind, whilst all the time respecting the accumulated insights preserved in Scripture and tradition.

One aspect of modern physics which has caught the eye of some theologians is the development of field theory. The scientific story begins with Faraday and Maxwell in the nineteenth century, and the subject has burgeoned in our own day. All established modern accounts of the structure of matter are quantum field theories. A field is an extended system, taking values at all points of space and instants of time. This omnipresent character has fired the imagination of some theologians. In the history of ideas, Faraday's use of field theoretic ideas has been seen as a turning away from mechanical and atheistic notions of 'atoms and the void'. But the theologians seem to go further.

Wolfhart Pannenberg has written that

> field theories from Faraday to Einstein claim a priority for the whole over the parts. This is of theological significance, because God has to be conceived as the unifying ground of the whole universe if he is to be conceived as the creator and redeemer of the world. The field concept could be used in theology to make the effective presence of God in every single phenomenon intelligible.[22]

These words occur in a section of his essay labelled 'Field and Spirit'. One seems dangerously close to Newton's equation of absolute space with the sensorium of God. Pannenberg believes that Newton was no pantheist but rather he 'took space as the medium of God's creative presence at the finite place of his creatures in creating them'.[23]

Another theologian enamoured of the field concept is Tom Torrance. He believes that Einstein presented us with a view of the universe as 'a unitary open system', and that from his attempts to construct a unified field theory, there emerged 'the concept of the continuous field of space-time which interacts with the constituent matter/energy of the universe, integrating everything within it in accordance with its unitary yet variable, objective rational order of non-causal relations'.[24]

The physicist does not feel instantly at home in this discourse. Metaphorically, a 'spiritual field' is no better or worse an image of divine presence than a 'spiritual gas' (or Stoic fine matter). They are ways of expressing spread-outness, together with (in the physical realizations) the presence of energy. Physically, a field does not of itself serve to loosen up nature. It is simply a dynamical system with an infinite number of degrees of freedom – that is, an infinite number of ways in which it can change – but these changes take place in a perfectly orderly fashion. Classical fields are determinate entities; the equations they satisfy are partial differential equations rather than ordinary differential equations, but that is not a critical distinction. Moreover, fields are local entities – that is to say I am perfectly free to bring about changes 'here' without any constraint from, or instantaneous effect upon, what is over 'there'. In that sense, they are collections of parts.

If theologians want a picture derived from modern physics which truly claims 'a priority for the whole over the parts', they should look to quantum theory, rather than to classical field theory. One example of collective behaviour is provided by quantum statistics – that is to say, the behaviour of assemblies of the same sort of particle. Because quantum mechanics does not permit us to picture the motion of individual particles, quantum entities which are identical are also indistinguishable. If I start off with an electron at A and an electron at B and end up with an electron at X and an electron at Y, that is all that I can say about what has happened. I cannot affirm, as I could for a classical system by following the details of its motion, that the electron which started at A is the one which ended up at X. This rather innocuous-sounding condition of indistinguishability has some surprising consequences.[25] It leads either to Fermi statistics, where the presence of a particle in a state bars any other particle from that state (the Pauli exclusion principle, which provides the basis underlying atomic structure), or to Bose statistics, where particles show the opposite tendency and tend to congregate in the same state (Bose condensation, the basis of the laser). Robert Russell has discussed the analogical potency of these ideas. He sees the role of Fermi statistics in atomic physics as showing how 'chance gives order its structure' and Bose condensation as adding 'a unitive factor to the structure making up our world'.[26]

Much the most striking unitary aspect of the quantum world is provided by what is commonly called the Einstein-Podolsky-Rosen, or EPR, effect.[27] Once two quantum entities have interacted with each other, the one retains a power to influence the other, however far apart they may subsequently separate. A measurement on one of the particles produces a collapse of their joint wavefunction which has an immediate consequence for the other particle. What is involved here is a genuine causal effect, bringing about an actual change in the state of the far particle (which may be, as we conventionally say, 'beyond the moon'). The EPR effect is not the unproblematic unveiling of a hitherto-unobserved but always-the-case aspect of that particle's motion (as could result from an act of classical measurement without its occasioning any perplexity), but rather it is the counterintuitive passion-at-a-distance (to use Abner Shimony's striking phrase)[28] which that distant particle undergoes as a result of my experimenting upon its partner here in the laboratory. That is what quantum theory asserts. It was clearly a matter of the highest importance to check if nature really agreed with it and actually exhibited this strange togetherness-in-separation, or non-locality. The way to put the matter to the test was shown by John Bell.[29] The technique is to make a series of paired measurements on two particles (in practice, photons) whose states have been linked together by interaction in the appropriate way,[30] and to study the correlations which exist between the results obtained with one photon and the results obtained with the other. Bell showed that, if the underlying theory

94

were purely local, with no strange effects at a distance, then there was a bound (the Bell inequality) on how closely correlated the results could prove to be. In certain circumstances, quantum theory (by virtue of its non-locality) predicted a violation of this bound. Delicate investigations, particularly by Alain Aspect and his collaborators, showed that the Bell inequality was indeed violated in just the way that quantum theory predicted. Whatever the microscopic world is, it cannot be a collection of local, separated, parts. The paradox of subatomic physics is that it cannot be treated atomistically. This peculiarity of quantum theory is intrinsic and it is not an artefact of some incomplete or hamfisted way of setting up the theory (as Einstein had hoped). David Mermin comments: 'It is not the Copenhagen interpretation of quantum mechanics which is strange, but the world itself.'[31] The inescapable web of complex interconnectivity present in the quantum world produces a picture which Russell has called 'nature as gossamer'.[32]

Talk of instantaneous interaction will provoke the alert reader to inquire how all this squares with relativity. Does not the latter insist that physical effects propagate only with the velocity of light or less? Aspect's experiment was, in fact, cleverly designed to exclude the possibility of such luminal, or subluminal, influences being the source of the effect he measured. All the same, we do not have a direct clash with special relativity. The reason is that the latter's prohibition is on the superluminal propagation of signals carrying usable information, and it turns out that this does not happen with EPR.

The Aspect experiment measures the polarization states of two photons in a long series of observations on a succession of photon pairs produced by the apparatus. Each set of successive measurements for the 'rightward-moving' photon or for the 'leftward-moving' photon, respectively, yields a random set of results for that photon's polarization, as quantum theory says it should. The togetherness-in-separation is only manifest when we compare the two sets of measurements and find that rightward and leftward results are correlated to a greater degree than strict locality allows. This correlation itself cannot be used to convey a message from right to left since it is only apparent on the left when we already know what has happened on the right (that is, we have already received a message from right to left!). In more picturesque and metaphorical language, a listener on the right hears a noisy chatter, a listener on the left hears a noisy chatter, and only someone (contrary to relativity) in instantaneous communication with both right and left could perceive the harmonies established between these apparently random sounds.

95

(I owe this image to Robert Russell.) Thus there is no strict contradiction of EPR with relativity.

All the same, one feels uneasy. The truce seems a little fragile. The more objective one's view of the quantum world, the more the situation seems fraught with possible difficulty.[33] That is why Bohm's theory (where the physical but not-directly-observable wave, encoding information about the whole environment, is the medium of non-locality) looks particularly vulnerable.

It is time to face squarely the question of how real the quantum world is. In view of its counterintuitive strangeness, would it not be best to take a positivist or instrumentalist stance and regard quantum theory as no more than a highly successful manner-of-speaking by which we are able to predict the statistical patterns of macroscopic phenomena, without committing ourselves to an ontological belief in the existence of such curious underlying microscopic entities? The deep-seated instinct of the physicist to hold to a critical realist account of his subject causes him to recoil from such a proposition.[34]

The prime question is that of the status of the wavefunction or, more generally, the status of the quantum state that it represents. The superposition principle, with the unpicturability that it implies, means that we cannot in conventional quantum theory interpret the quantum state in any naive everyday-objective sense. (That would only be possible if we adopted Bohm's strategy of divorcing wavefunction and particle, making the latter picturable and the former unobservable.) But equally, the wavefunction is treated by quantum physicists with a degree of seriousness which accords it a status going beyond that of mere calculational device. Roger Penrose has written:

> Despite the fact that we are normally only provided with probabilities for the outcome of an experiment, there seems to be something objective about a quantum-mechanical state. It is often asserted that the state-vector [wavefunction] is merely a convenient description of 'our knowledge' concerning a physical system – or, perhaps, that the state-vector does not really describe a single system but merely provides information about an 'ensemble' of a large number of similarly prepared systems. Such sentiments strike me as unreasonably timid concerning what quantum mechanics has to tell us about the *actuality* of the physical world.[35]

I would want to replace the word 'objective' by the wider word 'real'. I have written:

> The wavefunction is the vehicle of our understanding of the

quantum world. Judged by the robust standards of classical physical physics it may seem a rather wraith-like entity. But it is certainly the object of quantum mechanical discourse and, for all the peculiarity of its collapse, its subtle essence may be the form that reality has to take on the atomic scale or below.[36]

The quantum world has its own nature of reality. Heisenberg[37] encouraged the thought of the wavefunction as being the carrier of potentiality (the superposition of a variety of outcomes) in contrast to its representing the instantiation of a definite state of affairs. Our difficulty in feeling quite at ease with this notion stems from our ignorance of how that general potentiality becomes a particular actuality as a result of observation – in other words, how the quantum world can be understood to interlock with the everyday world, without our having to embrace the crude and unsatisfactory dualism of the original Copenhagen interpretation. We return once more to the central quantum conundrum, the measurement problem. Until we have agreement on how to deal with that issue we shall remain in perplexity about detailed questions of quantum ontology. Options will vary from the many-worlds view that the wavefunction is all (so that Hawking and Hartle can even, in a highly symbolic and speculative way, write down 'the wavefunction of the universe' as the 'answer' to everything),[38] to the Bohmian claim that the wavefunction is just a veiled part of objective reality (an 'implicate order').[39] As so often, I find myself thinking that the truth is likely to be found somewhere between the two extremes. That would correspond to a solution of the measurement problem along the lines of possibilities (iv) or (v) discussed above (pages 90-2). In the absence of precise proposals it is difficult to say much more. Such an approach would seek to link together the microscopic and the macroscopic in an integrated account of physical reality. How it did so would constrain the manner and extent to which it could be said that quantum theory ties together observer and observed. Certainly there would be a relationship more interactive than that of the detached observer of classical physics, but it is by no means clear that one would have the kind of situation described by the wilder flights of an alleged 'observer-created reality'. The more modest phrase of an 'observer-influenced reality' would be a more appropriate account. In fact, the very idiosyncrasy of the quantum world reminds us of its stubborn, if subtle, facticity, over against us. If we take one of the criteria of reality to be its nature 'as that which we bump into' – that which resists our attempt to mould it to our prior expectation – then the quantum world asserts its reality by its very opposition to our common-sense expectation.

I believe that another powerful reason for taking the reality of quantum entities seriously is that the quantum world is intelligible, even if our understanding of it is not yet perfect. When the notion of an entity like an electron serves to make sense of great swathes of experience which without that notion would simply baffle us, then we have very good reason for believing in the existence of that entity. I have written elsewhere:

It is our ability to understand the physical world which convinces us of its reality, even when, in the elusive world of quantum theory, that reality is not picturable. This gives physics a good deal in common with theology as the latter pursues its search for an understanding of the Unpicturable.[40]

People sometimes feel that in a scientific age the doctrines of traditional Christian theology need remodelling and simplifying to bring them into line with 'what an educated person might be expected to be able to accept'. The counterintuitive ideas of the Trinity and the incarnation had best be replaced by notions less demanding and more in accord with everyday expectation – the general idea of a Mind behind things, and of Jesus as an inspiring figure or as a 'new emergent', spearheading the further upward march of evolutionary history. Scientists themselves are unlikely to accord so great an influence to the somewhat banal categories of everyday thought. They have learnt that the world is strange beyond our prior expectation, but also rationally satisfying in its idiosyncrasy. The doctrines of a tripersonal God and of his making himself known in human terms, have about them those elements of surprise and intellectual profundity which are characteristic of the best scientific theory. Our investigation of the physical world has stretched our minds and enlarged our notions of the conceivable. It would be surprising indeed if the encounter with God did not do the same.

I am not saying anything as ridiculous as asserting that after quantum theory anything goes. That theory's novel insights were only embraced after much struggle, rationally motivated by the need to respond to the stubborn way things are. I believe that theology is engaged in an analogously demanding attempt to do justice to our encounter with the Otherness of the divine nature (Chapter 1). I simply say that our experience of the quantum world prepares us for accounts of reality which will submit to no undue tyranny of common sense but which will seek, however difficult the task, to respect the nature of that with which we have to deal.

8 The Fall

If I were asked what is the major Christian doctrine that I find most difficult to reconcile with scientific thought, I would answer: the Fall. I do not mean the status of humankind as sinful. It seems only too clear that something is awry in the lives of men and women; that there is an innate bias frustrating good intentions and tarnishing hopes. Someone once said that original sin was the only experimentally verifiable Christian dogma! Even less do I mean the Christian diagnosis that this state of affairs arises from an alienation from God, the attempt to live autonomous lives by those who are by nature spiritually dependent upon the grace of their Creator. These insights seem to me to be plausible and illuminating.

The difficulty arises from picturing this situation as having arisen subsequent to an unfallen state, with the associated notion that a radical change occurred as the consequence of some disastrous ancestral act. Paul speaks of the way that 'sin came into the world through one man and death through sin, and so death spread to all men because all men sinned' (Romans 5.12). How does this square with our knowledge that *homo sapiens* evolved from more primitive hominids, which themselves evolved from preceding animal life and ultimately from the inanimate shallow seas of early Earth, and that death was always present in the animal world? We detect no sign of a sharp discontinuity in the course of earthly or cosmic history, no indication of a golden age from which our present plight descends by degeneration.

We have, I think, to make a clear distinction between the presence of physical evil and the presence of moral evil. The former is the inevitable consequence of a world exploring and realizing its own potentiality through the shifting operations of happenstance.[1] That world must contain impermanence as the ground of change, death as the prerequisite of new life. Its blind alleys and malfunctions will produce what humans perceive as the physical evil of disease and disaster. In that sense the universe is everywhere 'fallen' and it has always been so. The goodness of creation, seven times reiterated in Genesis 1, is to be understood in terms of fruitful potentiality (the Anthropic Principle) rather than initial perfection. Evolutionary cosmology is consonant with an Irenaean picture of growth into fulfilment, rather than an

Augustinian picture of decline from paradise.[2] Once such a world evolves to the point of containing self-conscious freely-choosing beings, it faces the possibility of a further 'fall' into moral evil, exemplified by lives of selfishness and rebellion. This, when it occurs, is then a new development in cosmic history, consequent on the new emergent of self-consciousness.[3]

The marvellously subtle story of Genesis 3 is not altogether inhospitable (under its mode of mythic discourse) to the accommodation of these insights. That something was troubled from the first is signified by the enigmatic presence of the serpent. Note that he is one of those 'wild creatures that the Lord God had made' (Genesis 3.1). There is divine responsibility for his presence. He is described as *'arum*, a word used in the Wisdom literature with the sense of 'prudent', acting in accord with the ambiguous way the world is (e.g. Proverbs 22.3). Is it altogether too fanciful to see him as partly a figure of the way things are, including in that the presence of physical evil? The Fall itself is pictured as a 'fall upwards'. The eating of the fruit from 'the tree that was desired to make one wise' (Genesis 3.6) is a symbol of emergent human faculties. Of course, we do not today picture this emergence as happening in a single act; it would have evolved, often gradually but perhaps sometimes saltationally. The cursing of the ground to which man must return in death (Genesis 3.17-19) is not the abrogation of a previous immortality and a prior unlimited fertility, but the dawning recognition of the quality of natural events. Physical evil had always existed but it had not been perceived *as evil* until humanity's appearance (just as Paul said the sin was not recognized as sin before the experience of the Law made its nature manifest (Romans 5.13)). Thus we can understand that sin and 'death' (the recognition of mortality) came together with the emergence of self-consciousness. The geneticist Dobzhansky asks of the human consciousness of death 'is this the evolutionary acquisition corresponding to the biblical symbol of Fall?'[4] My answer would be, only partially. The Fall has a moral significance lying deeper than the recognition of this world's transience.

The fundamental aspect of the Fall is the moral act of the rebellious refusal of creaturely status, the desire 'to be like God' (Genesis 3.5). How that came about we do not know. It is clearly present in us today, transmitted culturally and even, conceivably, partly genetically (sociobiology is not the whole human story but it may be part of that story). On the view I am proposing, the whole universe is fallen physically but only part is fallen morally. If there are other life-bearing planets elsewhere in the cosmos it is conceivable that their inhabitants may be as innocent of moral evil as were the dwellers in C. S. Lewis's *Perelandra*.[5]

Is all this over-ingenious eisegesis, the reading in of what was never there in an unnecessary attempt to reinterpret an ancient tale that would be better discarded? I certainly offer these interpretations with an appropriate degree of tentativeness. Nevertheless it is an exercise I wish to attempt – to see what degree of coherence I can find between past tradition and present understanding in this rather extreme test case. Wrestling with the early chapters of Genesis has been going on for centuries with varying results – in Paul, in the Fathers, and so on to the present day. Liberals may find the discussion fantastically archaic, conservatives may find it dangerously speculative, but for me it is a kind of practical appendix to the general argument of Chapter 5. There are two further issues it must face.

The first is the extent to which the Fall has defaced the image of God which Genesis 1.26-7 pictures as the Creator's gift to humanity. The question is one that has given rise to much exegetical dispute, concerning the nature of the 'image' and the 'likeness', and also concerning the degree of their defacement. I simply wish to make one comment. The success of science in reading the Book of Nature, and more generally the success of the strategy of wagering on the rationality of the world (as advocated in Chapter 1), encourages the thought that humanity is not wholly benighted in the exercise of its rational faculties. We can indeed believe that there is a 'true light that enlightens every man' (John 1.9). One consequence of that is the validity of attempting the rational inquiry of natural theology.[6]

The second issue is more perplexing. The biblical tradition speaks not only of a Fall but also of its reversal, a time when 'the wolf shall dwell with the lamb and the leopard shall lie down with the kid' (Isaiah 11.6) in a return to Eden. This prophetic theme is taken up in the New Testament concept of a 'new creation' (2 Corinthians 5. 17), 'a new heaven and a new earth... where death shall be no more, neither shall there be mourning nor crying nor pain, any more, for the former things have passed away' (Revelation 21.1-4). In language appropriate to their times, these verses are expressing a hope extended beyond humanity to assume universal proportions. It is the same hope so remarkably expressed by Paul when he said that 'the creation itself will be set free from its bondage to decay and obtain the glorious liberty of the children of God' (Romans 8.21). Only a hope of this cosmic scope would be worthy of God the Creator. He must have a purpose for all that he has brought into being and nothing of good can finally be lost. Men and women are given the Christian hope of resurrection, a destiny beyond death involving the re-embodied existence necessary for psychosomatic unities like ourselves, but within a new environment of God's choosing. That environment – the new heaven and the new earth – must surely be envisaged as being the destiny also of the whole universe, otherwise condemned to collapse or decay.[7] The vast tracts of the cosmos are not to be considered as merely disposable accessories to the local human story of Earth. Genesis 1 reiterates that *all* that was made was 'good'.

To speak in this way does not imply the necessary re-creation of everything that was. The anaerobic unicellular life of early Earth was a staging post of biological evolution and we do not have to suppose that it, as such, must reappear somewhere in the new heavens and the new earth. Its good will be sufficiently preserved in a continuing destiny for that to which it gave rise.

The problem that we face is, how could this hope be a coherent hope? How could the new creation avoid being at least a partial rerun of the old? We can just imagine how a process of spiritual purgation and healing brought about by the operation of God's grace will bring to an end human sinfulness by the creation of a redeemed community in Christ, so that moral evil is excluded from the world to come (see Revelation 21.8; the image of the 'second death' is a symbol of the impermanence of the evil that is in each of us, its necessary ultimate deletion). But how could such a world be free from physical evil, which we have stated to have been always present in the world as a consequence of the mode of operation of physical process? How can there be a world with no more pain or death? And if the laws of matter could be revised in such a way as to exclude physical evil, why did not the Creator ordain just those laws the first time round, rather than bothering with the old unsatisfactory variety? In short, if the world to come is to be physically 'unfallen', why was that not true of this world also?

I think that the answer lies in that patient *creatio continua*, creation-through-process, which is the way of a loving Creator in his dealings with a creation to which he has given the gift of freedom. The pattern of present physical process represents that good which God in his wisdom bestows on a universe allowed to exist over against him and permitted to make itself through the realization of its own fruitful potentiality. The good that is possible in the new creation is a different good, for it is based on the coming-to-be of a different relationship between God and the world. In the astounding symbol of the Cosmic Christ (especially in Colossians 1.15-20) we have the image of a reconciliation of universal scope, so that the new creation comes about – in a way unimaginable to us in its mystery – through a relinquishment of that gift of independence and a return, through Christ, to a more intimate relationship with the Father of All. Involved here is the concept of the eventual solidarity of all that is in the Cosmic Christ – 'all things were created through him and for him. He is before all things and in him all things hold together' (Colossians 1.16-17). We are taken far beyond notions of the Church as Christ's Body, to a holistic vision of immense scope, of which the togetherness-in-separation of quantum theory (p. 94) and the place of the material elements in the Eucharist are, in their very different ways, elementary hints. A sacramental destiny awaits the universe.[8]

The new creation represents a state attainable only through that act of the return by the present creation. It represents, not the replacement of the world, but its redemption. Gabriel Daly says: 'The word "new" could mislead here. It does not imply an abolition of the old but rather its transformation. It is a "new creation" but, unlike the first creation, it is not *ex nihilo*. The new creation is what the Spirit of God does to the first creation.'[9] The new creation is not *ex nihilo* but rather *ex vetero*. These ideas are certainly not easy but I believe that we have to struggle with something like them if we are to embrace a true and lasting hope. One thinks of the way the Eastern Church speaks of deification as the destiny of creation. 'The world was created from nothing by the sole will of God – this is its origin. It was created in order to participate in the fullness of the divine life – this is its vocation.'[10] Above all one thinks of the empty tomb, with its proclamation that the risen Lord's glorified body is the transmutation of his dead body; that in Christ there is a destiny not only for humanity but also for matter. In fact, the emptiness of the tomb is delivered from being the act of a divine conjuror precisely because it is the anticipation within history of that which awaits all beyond history. It is no arbitrary act but it is of a piece with the purposes of God. Christ is 'the first born from the dead' (Colossians 1.18), 'the first fruits of those who have fallen asleep' (1 Corinthians 15.20).

These are deep matters of which I cannot pretend to a full understanding. The thoughts are speculative, but if we are to take cosmology and creation and hope with appropriate seriousness I think this will demand something like the counterintuitive complexity at which my jejune remarks are hinting. I offer the discussion simply as an exercise in attempting to hold together the insights of science and the Christian tradition, both of which

I wish to respect, for I believe that both are essential components in the search for truth and understanding, necessary parts of the engagement of reason with reality.

Notes

Introduction

1 Polkinghorne (1986), a general introduction; (1988), concerned with natural theology, creation, and the nature of reality; (1989a), concerned with God's interaction with the world and problems of theodicy and prayer.

2 cf. Ford (1989), a two-volume survey of twentieth-century systematic theology containing virtually no reference to the interaction of science and theology.

3 Torrance (1969) and subsequent writings.

4 Park (1988).

5 Barton (1988).

1 Rational Inquiry

1 Carnes (1982), p. 54.

2 Barbour (1974), ch. 7.

3 Kuhn (1970).

4 See Newton-Smith (1981), ch. 4. See also Murphy (1990).

5 See Polkinghorne (1989b).

6 Barbour (1974), p. 135.

7 Peacocke (1984), p. 51.

8 Polkinghorne (1986), p. 42.

9 Torrance (1969), pp. 130-1.

10 Lonergan (1973), p. 265.

11 ibid., p. 14.

12 Pannenberg (1976), p. 303.

13 For surveys of the issues, see Leplin (1984); Newton-Smith (1981).

14 Polkinghorne (1989b), ch. 21.

15 As alleged in Pickering (1984).

16 In Leplin (1984), p. 29.

17 ibid., p. 30.

18 Park (1988), p. 231.

19 Ricoeur (1970), p. 351.

20 Polanyi (1958), p. 214.

21 ibid., p. 315.

22 See Polkinghorne (1979), ch. 6.

23 Polanyi (1958), p. 299.

24 See Barnes (1974), pp. 27-31; Polanyi (1958), pp. 287-94.

25 See Leggett (1987), ch. 4.

26 Hawking (1988), p. 175.

27 Bohm (1980).

28 Sykes (1984), pp. 51-2.

29 Polkinghorne (1984), ch. 8.

30 See Polkinghorne (1988), ch. 2.

31 Lonergan (1958), p. 672.

32 Carnes (1982).
33 Puddefoot (1987), p. 16.
34 Einstein (1954), p. 233.
35 MacIntyre (1988), p. 173.
36 Lindbeck (1984), p. 130.
37 ibid., p. 18.
38 ibid., p. 128.
39 ibid., p. 134.
40 ibid., pp. 68-9.
41 ibid., p. 16.
42 ibid., p. 40.
43 Newton-Smith (1981), pp. 162-4.
44 See Ward (1987).
45 Quoted in Tracy (1981), p. 421.
46 See Carnes (1982), ch. 7.
47 Reprinted in Gill (1987), p. 94.
48 See also Bohr (1958), pp. 32-66; Polkinghorne (1984), ch. 5.
49 Torrance (1969), pp. 9-10.
50 Mitchell (1973), p. 19.
51 Ramsey (1957), p. 38.
52 Ramsey (1964), p. 60.
53 Ramsey (1957), p. 79.
54 Frye (1982), p. 67.
55 Ramsey (1957), pp. 14-15.
56 Lonergan (1973), p. 240.
57 Barbour (1974), p. 136.
58 Soskice (1985), p. 150.
59 Tracy (1981), p. 125.
60 Wainwright (1980), p. 201.
61 Hardy and Ford (1984); Wainwright (1980); see also Sykes (1984), ch. 11.
62 Wainwright (1980), p. 361.
63 ibid., p. 275.
64 Ramsey (1957), p. 85.
65 ibid., p. 63.
66 Dix (1945), p. 744.
67 Otto (1923).
68 James (1960), lectures 16 and 17.
69 See also Murphy (1990), ch. 5.

2 Rational Discourse
1 See, for example, Polkinghorne (1989b).
2 Quoted in Ramsey (1964), p. 2.
3 Lonergan (1973), pp. 284-5.
4 Barbour (1974), p. 6.
5 ibid., p. 38.
6 Peacocke (1984), p. 42.
7 Soskice (1985), p. 55.
8 See Polkinghorne (1979), ch. 5.
9 Bohr (1958).
10 MacKay (1988), chs 1 and 3.

11 ibid., p. 35.
12 Barbour (1974), p. 78.
13 One could say the same of configuration space (Where are you?) and momentum space (What is going on?) in quantum theory.
14 Polkinghorne (1988), ch. 5.
15 Barbour (1974), pp. 84-91.
16 Quoted by Farmer (1935), p. 173.
17 Polkinghorne (1986), pp. 45-7; (1988), ch. 2.
18 Barbour (1974), p. 30.
19 Soskice (1985), p. 99.
20 Wilczek and Devine (1988), p. 215.
21 Soskice (1985), p. 15.
22 ibid., p. 133.
23 Frye (1982), p. 7.
24 McFague (1987), p. 33.
25 Ricoeur (1978), p. 288.
26 Farrer (1948), p. 119.
27 C. D. Lewis, quoted in Dillistone (1955), p. 22.
28 Soskice (1985), p. 153.
29 Frye (1982), p. 56.
30 McFague (1987), p. 16.
31 Quoted in Brown (1987), p. 179.
32 Farrer (1948), pp. 44-5.
33 Tillich (1957), p. 45.
34 Quoted in Ihde (1971), p. 164.
35 See Polkinghorne (1989a), pp. 94-6.
36 P. Tillich, quoted in Dillistone (1986), p. 124.
37 Quoted ibid, p. 135.
38 Rahner (1975), p. 122.
39 Dillistone (1986), p. 135.
40 Brown (1987), p. 67.
41 Tillich (1957), p. 50.
42 Monod (1972).
43 Polkinghorne (1986), pp. 50-55.
44 Atkins (1981).
45 Quoted in Barbour (1974), p. 24.
46 Carnes (1982), p. 118 (my italics).
47 Polkinghorne (1988), p. 97.
48 McFague (1987), pp. xi-xii.

3 The Nature of Reality

1 Peacocke (1986), p. 28.
2 Peacocke (1979), ch. 4; (1986), chs 1 and 2.
3 Polkinghorne (1986), ch. 6.
4 Weinberg (1977).
5 Davies (1989), ch. 12; Gleick (1988); Stewart (1989).
6 The variable x is the actual population divided by its maximum possible value.
7 Gleick (1988), p. 8.
8 This discovery of universal behaviour introduced a new natural constant into mathematics, the Feigenbaum number, 4.669...

9 Stewart (1989), p. 208.
10 See Gleick (1988), pp. 221-32; Stewart (1989), pp. 236-41.
11 See Peitgen and Richter (1986).
12 One important mathematical feature of the new dynamics is that its equations are usually non-linear.
13 Prigogine and Stengers (1984); see also Polkinghorne (1988), ch. 3.
14 Prigogine and Stengers (1984), p. 300.
15 See Herbert (1985), ch. 8; Polkinghorne (1984), ch. 6.
16 One might have guessed that it was due to the linearity of the Schrödinger equation, but this does not seem to be the case; see Davies (1989), p. 369.
17 Davies (1989), p. 366. J. Ford's article contains a good account of the problem of quantum chaos.
18 Polkinghorne (1988), ch. 5.
19 Moltmann (1985), p. 163.
20 MacKay (1988), especially chs 5 and 6.
21 See, for example, Polkinghorne (1984), ch. 7.
22 d'Espagnat (1989).
23 ibid., p. 16.
24 ibid., p. 11.
25 ibid., p. 210.
26 Polkinghorne (1988), ch. 4.
27 See ibid., pp. 79-82.
28 Polkinghorne (1989a).
29 See ibid., pp. 11-13.
30 ibid., ch. 2.
31 Peacocke (1986), p. 98.
32 There are connections here with Bowker's notion of religions as systems; see Bowker (1987), pp. 112-43.
33 See Cobb and Griffin (1976).
34 There are obvious connections with the dialectical theism of Macquarrie (1984).
35 See ref. 15.
36 Penrose (1989), pp. 296-9.

4 Reason and Revelation

1 Theissen (1984), p. 4; for a critique, see Polkinghorne (1988), pp. 87-8.
2 A useful phrase from Bowker (1987), ch. 2.
3 Polkinghorne (1984), p. 12.
4 See ibid., chs 2 and 3.
5 Feynman (1985).
6 See Wilzcek and Devine (1988), pp. 25-8.
7 Gardner (1983), pp. 209-10.
8 Atkins (1981).
9 Davies (1983); Montefiore (1985); Peacocke (1979); Polkinghorne (1988).
10 Polkinghorne (1988); chs 1 and 2.
11 See Barnes (1974); Feyerabend (1975); Kuhn (1970).
12 See Leplin (1984); Newton-Smith (1981); Peacocke (1984), ch. 1;

NOTES

Polkinghorne (1989b), ch. 21.
13 For a critique of Popper, see Newton-Smith (1981), ch. 3.
14 Gardner (1983), p. 209.
15 Polanyi (1958); see Polkinghorne (1989b), ch. 21.
16 See Polkinghorne (1983), pp. 17-19.
17 ibid., ch. 10.
18 ibid., ch. 9.
19 ibid., chs 6-8.
20 Buber (1970).
21 ibid., p. 112.
22 Polkinghorne (1988), pp. 1-3.
23 Lash (1988), p. 7.
24 Brown (1985), p. 16.
25 Lash (1988), p. 168.
26 ibid., p. 249.
27 ibid.
28 See Barnes (1974).
29 The motion would be chaotic; see Stewart (1989), pp. 66-7.
30 Lash (1988) criticizes William James's approach to religious experience as being elitist, but it is quite possible to build a case without appealing solely to the spiritual masters.
31 Hardy (1979).
32 Pafford (1976), p. 8.
33 Lash (1988), p. 115.

5 The Use of Scripture
1 Barton (1988), p. 18.
2 ibid., p. 21.
3 ibid., p. 40.
4 Quoted in ibid., p. 42.
5 J. D. Crossan, quoted in Soskice (1985), p. 109.
6 Frye (1982), p. 60.
7 Polkinghorne (1983), ch. 6.
8 See Dodd (1971).
9 Barton (1988), p. 49.
10 That is, if we follow the most likely chronology based on John. The well-known fact that John and the Synoptics agree that Jesus was crucified on a Friday but disagree on how the day was related to the Passover, tells us something about Scripture's relation to matters of historical detail.
11 Nineham (1976).
12 Soskice (1985), p. 152.
13 Lash (1986), p. 65.
14 Quoted in Lonergan (1973), p. 161.
15 Tracy (1981), pp. 7 and 13.
16 Barton (1988), p. 63.
17 Tracy (1981), p. 163.
18 Childs (1979); (1984).
19 Dunn (1977).
20 Barton (1988), p. 57.
21 ibid., p. 20.

22 For a sympathetic account of typology, seen as an expression of God's faithfulness, see Charity (1966).
23 Frye (1982), p. 220.
24 ibid., p. 221.
25 See Torrance (1969).
26 Barton (1988), p. 19.
27 Farrer (1948), p. 134.
28 Barton (1988), p. 30.
29 ibid., p. 59.
30 Polkinghorne (1988), pp. 3-6.
31 One is impressed by the absence of such embarrassing detail as one finds in the *Enuma Elish* (the Babylonian myth with which Genesis is often compared), where Marduk slices the defeated Tiamath in two, forming earth and sky of the two halves.
32 See Peters (1989).

6 Cross-Traffic
1 Hooykaas (1972); Jaki (1978); Russell (1985).
2 Polkinghorne (1988), p. 1.
3 Lonergan (1958), p. 684.
4 E. P. Wigner, Comm. in Pure and Appl. Math., 13 (1960), pp. 1-14.
5 Barrow and Tipler (1986); Leslie (1989).
6 Barrow and Tipler (1986), pp. 16-23.
7 The 'many worlds' of this interpretation properly refer to different outcomes of quantum measurement, not to differing basic law and circumstance.
8 Hawking (1988), pp. 140-1.
9 Moltmann (1981); (1985).
10 One reason for believing in the empty tomb is that its picture of the risen Lord's glorified body being the transmutation of his dead body, speaks to us of a destiny for matter as well as humanity.
11 Dyson (1979), ch. 21; (1988), ch. 6.
12 Barrow and Tipler (1986), ch. 10; F. J. Tipler in Russell *et al.* (1988), pp. 313-31.
13 Monod (1972), p. 110.
14 Polkinghorne (1988), ch. 4.
15 ref. 9.
16 Vanstone (1977), p. 63.
17 Polkinghorne (1989a), pp. 66-7.

7 Quantum Questions
1 Technically, the Galilean group of invariance is replaced by the Poincaré group (special relativity) or the group of general coordinate transformations (general relativity). Moreover, relativity theory has its own absolute (proper time), as has often been pointed out.
2 Macquarrie (1981), p. 242.
3 Barbour (1966), p. 315.
4 Capra (1975); Zukav (1979).
5 Polkinghorne (1986), pp. 82-3; (1988), pp. 93-4.
6 Dirac (1958), ch. 1; see also Polkinghorne (1984), ch. 3.

NOTES

7 See, for example, Polkinghorne (1984), ch. 4.
8 Swinburne (1977), p. 67.
9 For a critical account, see Gibbins (1987).
10 See, for example, Polkinghorne (1984), ch. 6.
11 Bohm (1980).
12 This dichotomy led Bohm to his notion of explicate and implicate orders; see ref. 11.
13 Bohm's answer is that the wave is a wave of information. But it has physically causal consequences, corresponding to what Bohm calls 'active information'.
14 For a more sympathetic view, see Bell (1987).
15 See, for example, Herbert (1985), pp. 172-5; Polkinghorne (1984), pp. 67-8.
16 Lockwood (1989), p. 226.
17 Hawking (1988), ch. 8; C. J. Isham in Russell et al. (1988), pp. 375-408.
18 See Bell (1987), ch. 22.
19 Even with a significant null result (the counter did not click), the record that this was so is irreversibly located in the past.
20 Bohr (1958), pp. 32-66.
21 Penrose (1989), p. 366.
22 In Peters (1989), p. 164.
23 ibid., p. 168.
24 In Peacocke (1981), pp. 90 and 92.
25 See, for example, Polkinghorne (1984), pp. 38-40.
26 In Russell et al. (1988), p. 364.
27 See, for example, Bell (1987); Herbert (1985), ch. 11; Polkinghorne (1984), ch. 7; and a particularly engaging account by N. D. Mermin in Cushing and McMullin (1989), pp. 38-59.
28 Quoted in Cushing and McMullin (1989), p. 77.
29 See ref. 27. For reformulation under somewhat less restrictive conditions, see J. P. Jarrett in Cushing and McMullin (1989), pp. 60-79.
30 Technically, they are in a singlet state.
31 In Cushing and McMullin (1989), p. 58.
32 In Russell et al. (1988), p. 357.
33 Cushing and McMullin (1989).
34 For a defence of critical realism in elementary particle physics, see Polkinghorne (1989b), ch. 21.
35 Penrose (1989), p. 268.
36 Polkinghorne (1984), p. 81.
37 Heisenberg (1959).
38 Hawking (1988), ch. 8.
39 Bohm (1980).
40 Polkinghorne (1986), p. 47.

8 The Fall

1 Polkinghorne (1989a), ch. 5.
2 Hick (1966).
3 An imaginative account of how this might have happened is given by J. F. Ross (McMullin (1985), p. 242). He pictures self-conscious-

ness being triggered by the otherness of first encounter with God and leading to a calamitous 'recognition of God as opposed self. The first human act... was to reject the sovereignty of God's Will.'

4 Dobzhansky (1967), p. 79.
5 Lewis (1943).
6 Polkinghorne (1988), chs 1 and 2.
7 Polkinghorne (1989a), ch. 9.
8 I see the sacramental status of the universe as being eschatological rather than present; compare with Peacocke (1979), pp. 289-91, and the discussion of Polkinghorne (1989a), ch. 8.
9 Daly (1988), p. 100.
10 Lossky (1957), p. 112.

Bibliography

Atkins, P. W. (1981) *The Creation*, W. H. Freeman

Barbour, I. G. (1966) *Issues in Science and Religion*, SCM Press
(1974) *Myths, Models and Paradigms*, SCM Press

Barnes, B. (1974) *Scientific Knowledge and Sociological Theory*, Routledge and Kegan Paul

Barrow, J. D., and Tipler, F. J. (1986) *The Anthropic Cosmological Principle*, Oxford University Press

Barton, J. (1988) *People of the Book?*, SPCK

Bell, J. S. (1987) *Speakable and Unspeakable in Quantum Mechanics*, Cambridge University Press

Bohm, D. (1980) *Wholeness and the Implicate Order*, Routledge and Kegan Paul

Bohr, N. (1958) *Atomic Physics and Human Knowledge*, Wiley

Bowker, J. (1987) *Licensed Insanities*, Darton Longman and Todd

Brown, D. (1985) *The Divine Trinity*, Duckworth
(1987) *Continental Philosophy and Modern Theology*, Blackwell

Buber, M. (1970) *I and Thou*, T & T Clark

Capra, F. (1975) *The Tao of Physics*, Wildwood House

Carnes, J. R. (1982) *Axiomatics and Dogmatics*, Christian Journals

Charity, A. C. (1966) *Events and Their Afterlife*, Cambridge University Press

Childs, B. S. (1979) *Introduction to the Old Testament as Scripture*, SCM Press
(1984) *The New Testament as Canon: An Introduction*, SCM Press

Cobb, J. R., and Griffin, D. R. (1976) *Process Theology, An Introductory Exposition*, Westminster Press

Cushing, J. T., and McMullin E. (ed.) (1989) *Philosophical Consequences of Quantum Theory*, University of Nôtre Dame Press

Daly, G. (1988) *Creation and Redemption*, Gill and Macmillan

Davies, P. W. (1983) *God and the New Physics*, Dent
(ed.) (1989) *The New Physics*, Cambridge University Press

d'Espagnat, B. (1989) *Reality and the Physicist*, Cambridge University Press

Dillistone, F. W. (1955) *Christianity and Symbolism*, Collins
(1986) *The Power of Symbols*, SCM Press

Dirac, P. A. M. (1958) *The Principles of Quantum Mechanics* (4th edn), Oxford University Press

Dix, G. (1945) *The Shape of the Liturgy*, Dacre Press

Dobzhansky, T. (1967) *The Biology of Ultimate Concern*, New American Library

Dodd, C. H. (1971) *The Founder of Christianity*, Collins

Dunn, J. D. G. (1977) *Unity and Diversity in the New Testament*, SCM Press

Dyson, F. J. (1979) *Disturbing the Universe*, Harper and Row
  (1988) *Infinite in all Directions*, Harper and Row
Einstein, A. (1954) *Ideas and Opinions*, Crown
Farmer, H. H. (1935) *The World and God*, Nisbet
Farrer, A. M. (1948) *The Glass of Vision*, Dacre Press
Feyerabend, P. (1975) *Against Method*, Verso
Feynman, R. P. (1985) *QED*, Princeton University Press
Ford, D. (ed.) (1989) *The Modern Theologians* (2 vols), Blackwell
Frye, N. (1982) *The Great Code*, Routledge and Kegan Paul
Gardner, M. (1983) *The Whys of a Philosophical Scrivener*, Oxford University Press
Gibbins, P. (1987) *Particles and Paradoxes*, Cambridge University Press
Gill, R. (1987) *Theology and Sociology*, Geoffrey Chapman
Gleick, J. (1988) *Chaos*, Heinemann
Hardy, A. (1974) *The Spiritual Nature of Man*, Oxford University Press
Hardy, D. W., and Ford, D. F. (1984) *Jubilate*, Darton Longman and Todd
Hawking, S. (1988) *A Brief History of Time*, Bantam Press
Heisenberg, W. (1959) *Physics and Philosophy*, Allen and Unwin
Herbert, N. (1985) *Quantum Reality*, Rider
Hick, J. (1966) *Evil and the God of Love*, Macmillan
Hooykaas, R. (1972) *Religion and the Rise of Modern Science*, Scottish Academic Press
Ihde, D. (1971) *Hermeneutic Phenomenology*, Northwestern University Press
Jaki, S. (1978) *The Road of Science and the Ways to God*, Scottish Academic Press
James, W. (1960) *The Varieties of Religious Experience*, Collins
Kuhn, T. (1970) *The Structure of Scientific Revolutions*, Chicago University Press
Lash, N. (1986) *Theology on the Road to Emmaus*, SCM Press
  (1988) *Easter in Ordinary*, SCM Press
Leggett, A. J. (1987) *The Problems of Physics*, Oxford University Press
Leplin, J. (ed.) (1984) *Scientific Realism*, University of California Press
Leslie, J. (1989) *Universes*, Routledge
Lewis, C. S. (1943) *Perelandra*, Bodley Head
Lindbeck, G. A. (1984) *The Nature of Doctrine*, SPCK
Lockwood, M. (1989) *Mind, Brain and the Quantum*, Blackwell
Lonergan, B. (1958) *Insight*, Longman
  (1973) *Method in Theology*, Darton Longman and Todd
Lossky, V. (1957) *The Mystical Theology of the Eastern Church*, James Clarke
McFague, S. (1987) *Models of God*, Fortress Press
MacIntyre, A. (1988) *Whose Justice? Which Rationality?*, Duckworth
MacKay, D. M. (1988) *The Open Mind*, IVP
McMullin, E. (ed.) (1985) *Evolution and Creation*, University of Nôtre Dame Press
Macquarrie, J. (1981) *Twentieth Century Religious Thought* (revised edn.), SCM Press
  (1984) *In Search of Deity*, SCM Press

BIBLIOGRAPHY

Mitchell, B. (1973) *The Justification of Religious Belief*, Macmillan
Moltmann, J. (1981) *The Trinity and the Kingdom of God*, SCM Press
(1985) *God in Creation*, SCM Press
Monod, J. (1972) *Chance and Necessity*, Collins
Montefiore, H. (1985) *The Probability of God*, SCM Press
Murphy, N. (1990) *Theology in the Age of Scientific Reasoning*, Cornell University Press
Otto, R. (1923) *The Idea of the Holy*, Oxford University Press
Pafford, M. (1976) *The Unattended Moment*, SCM Press
Pannenberg, W. (1976) *Theology and the Philosophy of Science*, Darton Longman and Todd
Park, D. (1988) *The How and the Why*, Princeton University Press
Peacocke, A. R. (1979) *Creation and the World of Science*, Oxford University Press
(ed.) (1981) *The Sciences and Theology in the Twentieth Century*, Oriel Press
(1984) *Intimations of Reality*, University of Nôtre Dame Press
(1986) *God and the New Biology*, Dent
Peitgren, H-O., and Richter, P. H. (1986) *The Beauty of Fractals*, Springer
Penrose, R. (1989) *The Emperor's New Mind*, Oxford University Press
Peters, T. (ed.) (1989) *Cosmos as Creation*, Abingdon Press
Pickering, A. (1984) *Constructing Quarks*, Edinburgh University Press
Polanyi, M. (1958) *Personal Knowledge*, Routledge and Kegan Paul
Polkinghorne, J. C. (1979) *The Particle Play*, W. H. Freeman
(1983) *The Way The World Is*, Triangle
(1984) *The Quantum World*, Longman
(1986) *One World*, SPCK
(1988) *Science and Creation*, SPCK
(1989a) *Science and Providence*, SPCK
(1989b) *Rochester Roundabout*, Longman
Prigogine, I., and Stengers, I. (1984) *Order out of Chaos*, Heinemann
Puddefoot, J. (1987) *Logic and Affirmation*, Scottish Academic Press
Rahner, K. (1975) *A Rahner Reader* (ed. G. A. McCool), Darton Longman and Todd
Ramsey, I. T. (1957) *Religious Language*, SCM Press
(1978) *Models and Mystery*, Oxford University Press
Ricoeur, P. (1975) *The Symbolism of Evil*, Beacon Press
(1978) *The Rule of Metaphor*, Routledge and Kegan Paul
Russell, C. A. (1985) *Cross-Currents*, IVP
Russell, R. J., Stoeger, W. R. and Coyne, G. V. (ed.) (1988) *Physics, Philosophy and Theology*, Vatican Observatory
Soskice, J. M. (1985) *Metaphor and Religious Language*, Oxford University Press
Stewart, I. (1989) *Does God Play Dice?*, Blackwell
Swinburne, R. (1977) *The Coherence of Theism*, Oxford University Press
Sykes, S. W. (1984) *The Identity of Christianity*, SPCK
Theissen, G. (1984) *Biblical Faith*, SCM Press
Tillich, P. (1957) *Dynamics of Faith*, Allen and Unwin
Torrance, T. (1969) *Theological Science*, Oxford University Press

Tracy, D. (1981) *The Analogical Imagination*, SCM Press
Vanstone, W. H. (1977) *Love's Endeavour, Love's Expense*, Darton Longman and Todd
Wainwright, G. (1980) *Doxology*, Epworth Press
Ward, K. (1987) *Images of Eternity*, Darton Longman and Todd
Weinberg, S. (1977) *The First Three Minutes*, Andre Deutsch
Wilczek, F. and Devine, B. (1988) *Longing for the Harmonies*, Norton
Zukav, G. (1979) *The Dancing Wu Li Masters*, Rider

Index

INDEX

118

INDEX